Embracing (Cwtch-ing) Me, God and Others!

Glenn Miles PhD

Glenn M Miles PhD
Email: drglennmiles@gmail.com
facebook.com/drglennmiles
https://my book.to/embracingme

POWERFUL BOOKS

Published by Powerful Books.

ISBN 978-1-83522-044-3 (eBook)

ISBN 978-1-83522-046-7 (HC)

ISBN 978-1-83522-045-0 (PB)

Contents

Aknowledgements

There are so many people I want to thank for their support during different stages of my life. I am grateful primarily for my loving parents and children. I am grateful for my darling wife Siobhan. I am grateful for those in the church I grew up in who treated me with kindness, especially Tom and Marina Dodd, and Dave & Katy Hughes. I am grateful for my mentors over the years; John and Mary Benford, Dot and Mike Palmer-Fry, Carrie Herbert, Chris Matthews, and Cathy Hancock. I am grateful for my children's patience and acceptance of me. I am grateful for my friends at home and overseas, and at Linden church without whose support and acceptance of me I would not feel comfortable enough to write this book. I want to thank Perry Power and my author peers for their unfailing support too. I am grateful to a few friends who read a draft copy of this to provide me with previews, comments and suggestions.

Cover photo taken by Steve Mussell of Nice Smile.

Preface

"This book is for folk challenged with being/becoming their authentic selves in the face of rigid religious straightjackets. It's also for people who are working at the coalface of human rights addressing abuse and evil in our world." *- **Sharon Wilkinson, International Development Worker***

"Glenn has survived so much in his life on this earth. Yet he has also thrived and has emerged with more grace and love than almost anyone I have known. His vision and passion to advocate for and support other survivors and those who are vulnerable, has defined his life in Wales, the UK and around the world for the decades I have known him. Now, for the first time, he is telling his own story with raw vulnerability and honesty, giving insight into his experiences and in doing so, is speaking out, raising awareness and breaking down barriers, especially in the faith community, where silence and ignorance has often thrived. I hope these words inspire others to do the same." *- **Helen Sworn, Founder of Chab Dai International***

"*This book is a testament to just how far perseverance and faith can take you, even in the face of immense challenges. Through his unwavering honesty and humour, Glenn offers the reader hope found in unlikely places – and more than a few challenging insights along the way. If you need a reminder that you can get through just about anything and still make a beautiful difference in the world, this story is for you.*" **- Craig Greenfield, author of Subversive Jesus**

"*With disarming honesty and loving insight, Glenn navigates the grit and profound beauty of servant leadership. This book is a kaleidoscope of experiences, spanning continents, cultures, and causes. It weaves together personal struggles, professional challenges, and spiritual growth into a mosaic that reveals the complex nature of a life dedicated to serving others. A survivor in every sense of the word, Glenn's journey challenges and inspires readers to embrace their own truths with courage, humility, and compassion*". **- Jarrett Davis, Social Researcher & Consultant. Up! International. (Colleague of Glenn's for the past 12 years.)**

"*Across countries, disciplines, perspectives, and faiths, Glenn portrays the epic journey of his life with humility, honesty, and love. He opens up about his own challenges and learnings so that others may reflect and connect with him and his story. Rather than call out, Glenn calls in readers to join him in humanity and all the hardship, beauty, and messiness it entails.*" **- Madeline Stenersen, Psychologist and Social Researcher, St Louis University, USA**

"It's amazing that Glenn has packed so much into his life already. Some aspects are a challenging read and Glenn has a very gentle way to open up difficult conversations as well as being very open and vulnerable about his own shortfalls, and health struggles. Made me cry in places, made me laugh, made me smile and made me pray that Glenn would find a partner for the next chapter of life!" - **Frances J Charles, retired Systemic Psychotherapist and Social Worker (UK)**

"The Irish teacher and poet John O'Donohue penned a blessing for friendship that starts like this;

> "May you be blessed with good friends, And learn to be a good friend to yourself, Journeying to that place in your soul where there is love, warmth, and feeling. May this change you."

As I read Glenn's words in his autobiography I felt as though I was witnessing his soul be torn open and exposed, left vulnerable, in a way that is so rare today that it is uncomfortable to watch. I wanted to help him cover it and at times it was hard to read. After finishing his great chronicle, I now feel that I journeyed with him as he learned to be a good friend to himself. I traveled with him as he befriended and listened to ignored and forgotten people all over the world. I clearly saw him offer love and warmth to those who were suffering. This is an impressively authentic true story filled with adventure, adversity, and questioning. It is relevant to the modern reader in this disconnected world. Glenn has a lot to teach all of us by the way he changed and learned to show himself love. I am honored to call him a friend and thankful for the way his vulnerability encourages me to *journey to that same place in my own soul."* **- Samantha Miller, Director of Voices Heard LLC,** which offers Restorative Justice Facilitation and Training as well as Child Safety Consulting Worldwide.

"This book is profound in its simplicity. As Glenn says in his introduction the chapters are short, but you may need to take your time. Some stories are hard to read, even when they are rooted in anecdotes that are fun. I found myself racing through his easy, almost breezy, prose as if I was there with him in the relatable story—but then gasping with shock at the harmful turns it would suddenly take. And as I was overcome by the enormity of evil that we humans can inflict on each other (on purpose and unwittingly) I was also renewed by Glenn's narrative device of Survival, both in the titles of the chapters and in the experience of his real life. Glenn's story is particular to him and the times and places of his individual life. But it is also universal—to us and to the world around us. The resources he shares give us tools to recognize and navigate the things we as readers have had to survive and empower us to help others survive as well. I highly recommend this powerful work crafted by a person who has not only survived but thrived, again and again and again. Through his own stories of resilience he encourages us to the same." **- Christa Crawford, Co-editor of the 'Stop the Traffik' Trilogy.**

"This is a courageous account of an interesting life. Glenn writes with honesty and vulnerability, inviting the reader into the challenges and lessons of his eclectic experience. The story is encouraging to those at any stage of life, particularly those who feel marginalised and misunderstood. Glenn's journey speaks of survival and overcoming, and points to

resources to support others in their quest for 'survival'." - **Cath Hancox, Counsellor, Trainer and Supervisor, Trinity St. Davids University.**

"I loved reading Glenn's autobiography. I found his story incredibly touching and moving - we are all ordinary people and all have difficult challenges and I felt that Glenn highlights this beautifully. Glenn's open heart about his struggles with his own sexuality, the guilt and shame he has felt and his personal triumph in achieving his own sense of authenticity are extremely important. As a gay-identifying person myself, I fully understand this struggle, the toxic effect it places on one's own life and the inner fight for self-respect in a world where homophobia is rife. Even so, Glenn has still maintained his honest and truthful relationship with his faith and with God - we need to give this the space it deserves. Where faith and love are concerned we need to reflect upon our own human flaws. None of us are perfect but in the end, love is love; there is no doubt about it. The difficulties Glenn presents in his own self-esteem has actually been the making of this man who has done and continues to do good things with his life even though at times society and religion have cast a shadow upon the perfection of who he is as an individual. Bravo Glenn - your book and life will inspire many." - **Elbarace (Gay Elvis) nee James Andrew Haslam.**

"An autobiography that left me feeling incredulous at just how much can be packed into one life. Glenn recounts and reflects in an open and honest manner. This is not always a comfortable read. From damaging experiences during childhood and adolescence right through to the trauma of losing Siobhan, his soul-mate and best friend he does not hold back

from telling it like it was for him. Yet through it all what comes across is the tender-heartedness of someone who was prepared to be an advocate for some of the most vulnerable, someone who made himself available. And that's what he is still doing. It is a privilege to count him as a friend." - **Chris Matthews, Former Pastor at Linden Church, Swansea.**

"We are all travelling a path through life, and for many the direction of travel is unclear. For Glenn however it was clear early on that he would go to serve the people of Cambodia, and in particular the children. This was non-negotiable, and this book tells of his single-mindedness and determination to make this happen. As you read his story you can't help but reflect on the paradox in Glenn's life of selfless giving in the face of extraordinary challenge and trauma.....almost a case of 'you couldn't make this up'. Glenn's theme is 'survival'. This suggests to me 'he just made it, despite.......'. Knowing Glenn as I do, he more than survived his experiences, instead they enabled him to grow into the extraordinary person he is today. God sometimes sends 'angels' to reveal something of Himself to us. Glenn's wife Siobhan, was for me a truly remarkable person. From what I now know from this book, I believe she was an angel. What next? In a way, this book leaves an open question and one we don't know the answer to. I'm looking forward to the sequel." - **Paul Rowley, a friend for over 45 years.**

Chapter 1

Introduction

"I have learned now that while those who speak about one's miseries usually hurt, those who keep silent hurt more."
C.S. Lewis

T he Welsh have a beautiful word 'Cwych' which means a cuddle or embrace, with a sense of offering warmth and safety. When I talk about embracing in the title I mean that. I am learning to embrace myself, God and others in a kind of trinity where each corner of the triangle is necessary.

A Survivor is a person who "manages to continue or exist despite difficult circumstances". When I describe 'survived' I sometimes mean I survived going through it, for other things I survived because it was prevented from happening. I am grateful for the times when I felt God holding my hand in the challenges and other times when I felt God protecting me from a worse thing from happening.

Everyone's story is different and every perspective is

different. There is a metaphor where 6 blind people are put in front of an elephant and asked to describe what they feel. They are each feeling different parts of the elephant and feel different things; a spear (tusk), a hose (trunk), a fan (ears), a wall (side), a pole (leg), a rope (tail). This is my perspective on my story. Others may see things differently, but each person's understanding is valid.

Even a tragedy needs some humour. This is an eclectic biography, part life story, part resource guide, part story of abuse and overcoming. Some parts are hard to read. Other parts are fun.

I know that as a middle-class white man, I am privileged above and beyond what many people have to experience. Many people could only imagine having what I have. I have done and been to places some people only dream of.

However, I *have* experienced some challenges over the years, and by writing them down I hope to be able to process them and reflect on them as an adult. My reflections have helped *me* process what I have experienced but I hope it also helps others who are currently trying to deal with similar or much worse challenges. I am well aware that many people, because of their trauma are unable to tell their stories, but the voices of survivors need to be heard.

I have been able to write this autobiography because I have been part of a supportive community of people who have experienced abuse and who have become/are becoming authors. Perry Power is an extraordinary young man who has formed this group and is having enormous success in helping others to break the silence of abuse. I think I will be the 15th person who has written a Survivor Book.

Learning who I am has not always been easy. I have experienced my share of self-hatred over the years but going through this process has enabled me to be a little kinder to little me. When people read this I may lose my status as a good boy to some, but it is a relief to no longer have to hide parts of me. I am still me but more honest with myself and others.

I especially want this to be an encouragement and resource to people who have been sexually abused, particularly by people connected to the church who should have been protecting them. Telling my story might help them to tell theirs. I hope it will push churches to take their child safeguarding measures seriously.

I hope to be an encouragement to men in the church who have come out as gay— especially those who have done so later in life. As I write this biography, I am keeping a friend in mind and I am writing for him. He is coming out in his middle age and is struggling to believe that he can be Christian and Gay both equally at the same time. I believe that he and I can.

My story is about embracing myself because I feel embraced by God. It is about having the strength to go on because I feel God's embrace (cwyth) through my friends. Sometimes it's nice to feel an embrace (cwyth) with real arms.

Sadly, I think the global church needs to be held responsible both for what it has done and what it has not done. In theological terms, the sins of commission and omission. People are drawn to a church that is primarily loving and secondly inclusive. But many churches often reject this biblical mandate and make exceptions to whom Christ welcomes

I also want to encourage the churches in the Global North (West) to recognise our privilege and to invest our time, money and energy in helping our brothers and sisters in the Global South (Developing world) where the majority of Christians reside. It's crucial that we shift our focus from self-preservation and look outwards.

Some people prefer to just read a story. Others need research and resources to back up what is being said. This book has tried to do both and the research and resources are optional.

I am aware that I am someone who needs affirmation (probably too much). Losing my soul mate means that I no longer have a witness to acknowledge my life in the same way, so this is a way of remembering and sharing.

One night recently, I had a very visceral nightmare in which I was climbing a tall staircase holding a lamp. I was walking towards a light at the top, but crocodiles were biting my ankles and it hurt. When I reached down to my ankles my hand was bitten. I looked at my hand and I could see there were also large scars that had healed over, but they weren't disappearing. I long to be in the light. I believe that I am moving towards the light but the journey is sometimes long and hard.

Each chapter is short. But you may need to take your time. Some chapters may be hard to read. So this is a trigger warning to take care when reading. You can stop or miss chapters if you think they will be too hard to read. I have tried to write most of this consecutively but there may be a bit of time travel back and forth!

Resources:

- *Powerful Books* in case you want to write your biography of abuse too: <u>iamperrypower.com</u>

- My personal website for research and training: <u>gmmiles.co.uk</u>

Chapter 2

Surviving Prematurity

"Let's start at the very beginning. It's a very good place to start."
Do-Re-Me song from the ***Sound of Music***

I was a surprisingly strong baby. I was a survivor. I was born prematurely but even before that, my life was eventful. When I was just a few months old in my mother's womb, my mother had some pains so she sought help from the local doctor. He examined her and told her that she had lost her baby. Even though she had been bleeding she was not entirely convinced, so she went back to the doctor a few days later and when he examined her again he found that the baby (me) was still alive! The explanation she was given was that I had had a twin and that the twin had died and she had miscarried them. This is not as uncommon as I had thought and is called a 'vanishing twin'.

The doctor said that she needed to be on bed rest for the rest of the pregnancy to prevent me from being born too early, so my dad moved the bed downstairs and she did as she was told. At that time my mother, who was not a religious person, prayed to God that, if I survived, she would give me back to God in some way in the same way that Hannah dedicated Samuel to the temple. At the time she believed it helped me to be born premature but healthy. I think this later helped her to process my being away overseas for much of my adult life. She had given me back to God.

So, from the very beginning I experienced the grace of God. Challenges would come but God was always there.

The pregnancy progressed and I was born prematurely and spent my first few weeks in hospital. My older sister, Wendy, who was eight years older than me, was so thrilled to have a baby brother she wrote in her school textbook that she loved me so much and "would never leave me". Once she was taking me for a walk in the pram and some boys were teasing her for taking her doll out for a walk and then I cried out and they all ran away.

Wendy later had her own twins, who she had ten months after her first baby, giving her three babies in eleven months! What an amazing mother she turned out to be.

Reflection:

I have often wondered what it would have been like for my twin to have survived. Would we have been buddies/best friends? Would it have been a girl or a boy? Will I meet him/her in heaven? Would we have had similar lives or completely different ones?

Resource:

- Vanishing twin: <u>webmd.com/baby/what-is-a-vanishing-twin</u>

Chapter 3

Surviving Childhood and School

"Give me a child at seven and I will give you the man."
Aristotle, Greek Philosopher

After that start, in many ways, my childhood was very ordinary for an English boy. I lived in the suburbs, in a three-bedroom, semi-detached house. My parents were loving and I had an older brother and sister, and a younger sister who was adopted. Academically, I struggled during my school years, achieving five Ordinary levels, a GCSE grade of 1 and later one Advanced Level qualification.

As a young child my favourite toy was Jimmy Giraffe, a plastic giraffe with red wheels that I could pull along with a piece of string. Even now, I remember the taste of the string which I sucked for comfort. I also had a red teddy, a yellow bunny, and a koala bear that my dad got me from Australia. It had a baby and when you pulled it out from its mother, it would play 'Waltzing Matilda.'

I do remember that my parents were very loving despite the very challenging childhoods that they had experienced. My father had a very controlling grandmother who forced him to live with her as a young child whether he or his parents wanted him to. My father's father died when he was a teenager. My mother's father died before she was born, which led people to assume she was 'illegitimate'. They did not have social services available in those days so her mother just had to get to work as soon as possible even if it was cleaning public toilets. So mum was a latch-key kid who had to come home and look after herself whilst her mother worked.

My father worked in a London bank (Grindleys, which later became Australia New Zealand (ANZ) bank and later worked for the Bank of England. He commuted every day and worked hard. My mother was a very gifted 'jack/jenny of all trades' and did many part-time jobs, ensuring she was always home when we finished school so that we didn't have to live in the same way she did as a child. She hated cooking and told us she would give us pills if they were nutritious enough. Her culinary repertoire was limited but nutritious.

Something she would say that made us laugh as children was "You can have what you like to eat, there's beans!" meaning beans on toast the easiest food to cook. To this day my favourite meal is gammon, mashed potato, and baked beans! As a child, she was evacuated but loved the old lady who cared for her. But her mother called her home to London to earn money as a young teenager. One time her house was bombed when she was on a bus coming home. When the air raid sirens rang out, she fled into a bomb shelter. When she came out, smoke was rising from her home. Her mother was in the underground which acted as a bomb shelter. Although she was fine, she was worried about the dinner in the oven. The air raid warden went into what was left of the house and pulled out the dinner covered in brick dust. It was a moment of humour in a time of tragedy.

One way in which I learned to soothe myself was by sucking my thumb. When I was alone I would suck my thumb. It felt like I was in a safe place and I didn't have to think about being bullied at school. My brother didn't understand that and he knew that I was very self-conscious about my teeth that stuck out a little bit due to me sucking my thumb. To accentuate this he would deliberately knock my elbow so that it pushed my thumb up against my teeth. Then he would say to me, "Good, so now I've pushed your teeth out just that little bit more". Rather than stopping me from sucking my thumb, it encouraged me to do it even more as I sought to self-comfort. I also found it helpful to hide behind doors. I enjoyed the enclosed space and I could sit on the floor for ages sucking my thumb and feeling safe tucked behind the door in the dark. Of course, I occasionally shocked family members when they came in and switched the light on to find me hiding, but they assumed I was deliberately there to jump out on them!

I never really had a time as a young child when I believed God didn't exist. I just kind of knew he did. I felt him with me in the hard stuff. I didn't see the incongruity between science and faith. However it all started, God was still in it. I loved the beauty in nature, the aesthetics of art, and the intelligence of animals.

I was trying to remember my earliest memories of child-hood. At the end of the first day of school, I pulled the stool with steps just under the mirror to talk to myself. I climbed up and sat down to tell myself about my day. My mother later told me that I said to myself I didn't like school and I preferred to stay at home. Unfortunately, that wasn't a choice but it might have saved a lot of grief to stay home!

The classic stereotypical barber in the UK is one of the few places left which is exclusively male. As a non-masculine boy, going to the barber was awkward. How should I behave? Should I pick up and read the men's magazines? When he asked me what kind of haircut I wanted, I was tongue-tied. What was I supposed to say? Should I try to use a deeper voice?

Marion, a lady who my mum worked with took me to see a show of some kind. Mum had not been able to take me, so Marion offered to do so. She said to me recently that I was such a polite, good boy that she felt it was me who was taking *her* to the show. I made sure she had somewhere to sit and got her a cup of tea. I was a good boy, I was.

Reflection:

I realise now how much my parents overcame in their childhoods to provide a loving home for their children, and I am very grateful. I learnt the importance of a loving family and being kind. As an adult, my brother apologised to me and we are friends now.

Resource:

- School anxiety and refusal to go to school: <u>youngminds.org.uk/parent/parents-a-z-mental-health-guide/school-anxiety-and-refusal/</u>

Or scan me instead!

Chapter 4

Surviving Childhood Bullying by Peers

"It is our choices that show what we truly are, far more than our abilities."
Albus Dumbledore, Harry Potter books

O ne of my earliest memories was when a group of children my age (around 8 - 9 years) surrounded me in the cloakroom, pulled down my trousers and pants and laughed at my penis. I can't even remember what had led up to it or why they said they were doing it. It's rather strange to imagine why a group of children of around eight or nine would do such a thing but it happened and it emotionally hurt me. There wasn't much in the way of mental health care in those days for children.

I remember over many months, even years, I used to run to the children's toilets and throw up or at least retch and then go back to the class. I think the teachers and my parents thought it best to just ignore it in the hope it would go away. It didn't, but what could I do?

Bullying continued into secondary school. I remember there was a group of boys in my classroom and they would threaten me during lunch or break times. They would force me into a corner and then kick me and punch me. I was always covered in bruises but it was mostly covered up by my school uniform. Then they would threaten to beat me up after school. Sometimes I could escape through a hole in a hedge that surrounded the school. But other times it wasn't possible to escape them. I never felt safe at school. At that age, it felt like it was never, ever, ever going to stop.

I remember one woodworking teacher who was kind to me and he once said how brave I was. That helped me to know that one teacher cared, but I don't remember him ever telling the other boys to stop. Most of the teachers took little notice of the emotional pain that I was experiencing from bullying. I am pretty sure it affected my academic work as well as my feelings of self-worth.

One time in art class the teacher had to "do something" and left us on our own for an hour. I had recently seen a stallion mating with a horse so I decided to paint pictures of animals having sex. Lots of animals having lots of sex. I can only imagine if my picture reached the staff lounge for a good laugh afterwards but it surprisingly was never displayed at the school art exhibition.

I remember my mother asking me what was it about me that made them want to bully me? It was a very confusing question. It made me feel as if there was something wrong about me that needed correcting. I wondered if it was what I perceived as my high non-masculine voice, or the way that I spoke or the way I thought my teeth stuck out and had a gap between them. I wondered if it was mannerisms that I perceived to be effeminate. I didn't understand and I felt like, somehow, it was my fault. It seemed OK for someone like Larry Grayson or John Imman on the telly to be effeminate but not me.

As a sensitive boy, I was able to understand that it may well have been something tragic or difficult in the other boys' lives that made them act out their frustration in the violent way they did but, of course, that didn't help *me*.

One thing I did enjoy was the clubs that I was involved with in the evening. On Monday was *Boys Brigade* and later *St. Johns Ambulance Brigade,* Tuesday was *Animal Defenders,* Wednesday was *Wednesday Rally,* Thursday was *Junior Covenanters* (Jucos), Friday was youth group, Saturday was tap dancing classes and then Sunday was Sunday school of course. But even then I ended up leaving the *Boys Brigade* because of bullying. I was the first boy in the first Caterham division of the *Boys Brigade* and I had to leave because of bullying.

The leader tried to persuade me to come back. He came to my house but I didn't believe he could protect me from bullying and I didn't want to try it. So on Monday evenings, I joined St. John's Ambulance cadets and enjoyed that better anyway. One day I was happily running home from the cadets and was stopped by the police (the first and only time for me). They assumed that I was running away from something bad I had done, like breaking a window, and was up to no good. I wasn't arrested but it felt very disturbing to be accused of something I hadn't done, rather than enjoy the notoriety.

I mostly hung out with the two boys who coincidentally had exactly the same names (both called Stephen and their surnames (P) were also the same!). Interestingly, the three of us have since all come out as gay men. What do children sense in other children their own age that they feel threatened by? It is ironic in retrospect that children bullied us for being gay but they and I didn't know what that even meant.

Occasionally another boy, Chris, would sit with us in class. He was friendly but troubled. One day he admitted to us that his parents encouraged him to watch them when they were having sex. It seemed bizarre. It was hard to respond to. He was embarrassed. We were embarrassed. Then on Fridays after school, he said he would get a train to one of the London railway stations which I later found out to be a place where boys could get paid by adult men to sexually abuse them. It was possible his parents may have endorsed this, maybe even profited from it. As I look back on this I once again realise how common sexual abuse and exploitation is even in the seemingly uneventful suburbs.

I know my parents loved me, but they couldn't protect me all the time and they didn't know what to do about the bullying. Like many parents, they left it to the school but the school did nothing. I got very depressed about it and would get angry with myself for "being so stupid". I am sure it affected my school work and my self-esteem. As I thought about my 'wrong' sexual feelings I would find a place on my own and then would use my fist to punch my head again and again. I think it was a form of relief to feel pain. I didn't know about it at the time, but because I did this, I can identify with those who use self-cutting for the same reason.

In research I did in Cambodia on violence against children I included peer bullying, 45% of children said that it was extremely serious and this was alongside other types of violence such as sexual abuse.

Reflection:

So at seven years old I already had the heritage of a loving family. A secure, stable and safe home with clean water, central heating, and a good school. But I was already experiencing bullying at home and school that left me with a foundation of insecurity, low self-esteem, and fear of not being masculine enough, and in a church that I believe in retrospect overemphasised God's wrath of sin. I think the impact of bullying in childhood is underestimated. I think it can have a profound long-term impact on children. Parents need support to handle it well. I think it should be added to the Adverse Childhood Experiences list.

Resources:

- Research we did on bullying in Cambodia: gmmiles.co.uk/wp-content/uploads/2013/05/Summary-Part-1.pdf
- *National Bullying Helpline UK:* nationalbully-inghelpline.co.uk/kids.html

Chapter 5

Surviving Childhood Bullying by Teachers

"Bullying never has to do with you. It's the bully who's insecure."
Shay Mitchell

When I was around 12 years old the teacher who was in charge of P.E. (physical education) would call me Glenda and the other children would laugh. It was hurtful that the teacher, an adult, was effectively joining in with the bullying. The other P.E. teacher took me to one side one day and rubbed mud on my knees and face when I didn't want to join in the rugby game. He had no idea that getting dirty wasn't my problem at all. My problem wasn't getting dirty, I hated team sports with bully boys.

My female history teacher also bullied, teased, and humiliated me, and did not stop the other children when they picked on me in her classroom.

Despite the prohibition of corporal punishment in state

schools across the United Kingdom, there is growing recognition that certain forms of teacher bullying and mistreatment towards students persist. While physical punishment is explicitly forbidden, more insidious forms of psychological and emotional abuse continue to occur, often under the guise of disciplinary measures or classroom management.

One prevalent issue is the use of public humiliation as a means of asserting authority or control over students. Teachers may intentionally embarrass or ridicule pupils in front of their peers, subjecting them to unnecessary put-downs or unconstructive criticism that undermines their self-esteem and creates an intimidating learning environment. Such practices not only damage the student-teacher relationship but can also have long-lasting psychological impacts on the targeted individuals.

Furthermore, there have been reports of teachers regularly singling out and making examples of particular students in front of the class. This practice can create an atmosphere of fear and intimidation, where students feel constantly scrutinised and vulnerable to public shaming or ridicule. Such an environment is antithetical to fostering a positive and inclusive learning experience.

Perhaps most concerning are instances of personal comments or verbal abuse directed at students based on their appearance, sexuality, gender, disability, race, faith, or family background. Such discriminatory and derogatory remarks not only violate principles of respect and inclusivity but may also constitute forms of harassment or discrimination, with potentially severe legal and ethical consequences.

While the outright use of physical punishment has been outlawed, these more subtle forms of bullying and mistreatment by teachers can have equally damaging effects on students' well-being, academic performance, and overall educational experience. It is imperative that educational institutions and authorities take proactive measures to address and prevent such behaviours, fostering a safe and supportive learning environment for all students.

This kind of behaviour cannot be tolerated.

One time my English teacher decided we needed to understand sex more than the anatomy we were learning in the biology class. He read a poem to us about people who travelled on the top deck of a bus every day and didn't communicate with each other. Then they heard on someone's radio that there was an atomic bomb about to drop on everyone so everyone's inhibitions were put to one side and then all the passengers started having sex with each other on the bus. Then, of course, another announcement came that the bomb had been averted and that everyone could go back to what they were doing before. Every day after that when they got the bus the people on the top deck had an orgie.

This same teacher also told us what a homosexual was - a man who had a sexual relationship with men and women with women. It was the first time I had heard anything about this and I was fascinated. It didn't occur to me at the time that it applied to me. I was too busy trying to work out where homosexuals thought babies would come from if everyone became homosexual. I assumed that if you were gay you wanted everyone to convert to being one in the same way if you were a Christian, you wanted everyone to convert to one.

Another thing I remember was that my male art teacher, who had long hair and who was 'a bit of a hippy', was having a sexual relationship with one of the more 'mature' girls in our class. No one even considered that this was reportable. She seemed pleased with the notoriety it gave her but at 15 years she certainly wasn't old enough to consent.

I had an infatuation with my biology teacher. He was strong and handsome. He was also kind and didn't mind me asking questions. Fortunately, he did not feel the same way about me. I was sad when I heard his best friend was my Physical Education teacher who bullied me.

In research we have done with school children in Asia there is increasing evidence that teachers sexually abuse children, and not just male teachers. More needs to be done to stop this.

When it came to adult friends of my parents I did much better. I was part of a community choir that the church ran of mainly adults, and we would go to other churches to sing hymns. It was mostly fun except when Mum slipped on the ice and ended up with a broken wrist.

A couple in the church, John and Mary Benford, had a wonderful way of keeping their home open to young people. They provided a wonderful contrast to the teachers.

Reflection:

Considering how these teachers treated me, makes me angry. I was a vulnerable child who deserved respect. I am concerned that some teachers choose to do teaching because of the power differential that makes them feel important and respected but they don't understand that true respect comes from kindness.

Resources:

- *Bullying by Teachers - Advice for Parents and Caregivers:* kidscape.org.uk/advice/advice-for-parents-and-carers/talking-to-schools-about-bullying/bullying-by-a-teacher/
- Sexual abuse by teachers research: pure.hud.ac.uk/ws/portalfiles/portal/67011906/FINAL_THESIS.pdf

Chapter 6

Surviving Falling off the Wall

"Humpty Dumpty sat on a wall, Humpty Dumpty had a great fall. All the king's horses and all the king's men couldn't put Humpty together again."
British Nursery Rhyme

A s a young teenager, I had two recurring dreams. One was simply the colour pink; vivid deep Barbi pink. It just made me feel anxious and fearful for no apparent reason. In retrospect, I think it had to do with the fear of appearing too feminine. The other dream was me walking through a familiar alleyway but finding a secret exit that led to the sea. I loved the sea and even though it was not true it was a great escape into my imagination while it lasted.

I was an avid reader and read the Narnia stories by CS Lewis over and over again. I didn't always understand the allegories but it was Christian, so that was good enough for me.

One of my other forms of escapism was collecting things. I loved collecting badges/pins and had a great selection of shapes and sizes. Once I collected crisp/chip bags. If you cut out ten coupons on the corner of the pack then you could send it off and get a badge. I collected bags from all the bins in the local parks and sent hundreds and hundreds to the crisp/chip company. They sent me a huge bag of badges/pins and I was so happy even though they were plain and all the same.

I also longed for pets. I wasn't allowed a dog but I was allowed a hamster. I spent hours playing with 'Midas' and building tunnels for him. When he died (they only survived about two years) it was my first experience of grief. I was heartbroken. I buried him in the garden with a full ceremony. I got another hamster whom I called 'Cheeky' but I still missed Midas, the golden hamster.

One thing I was very grateful for was the school holidays and every summer my parents took us to the seaside somewhere. I was especially fond of knickerbocker glories and helter skelters (look them up on Google if you don't know what they are!). I remember one day when I was still very small walking along the sea wall on the promenade holding my dad's hand. It was high tide. I decided I wanted to walk on my own so I let go of Dad's hand but I must have slipped because I fell off the wall. My dad's reflexes were amazing and he caught me just as I was falling. When we went back to the same place the following day we realised just how high the wall was on the beach side and how far I would have fallen if I had fallen off. Phew!

One year we spent quite a bit of time on the pier in the amusement arcades where we could play video games. One game involved tanks blowing up things and I got quite good at it. In fact I scored better than my brother which he was not happy about. Most of the time if we played board games, for example, we had to play to the bitter end. I remember one time playing Monopoly with him and he wouldn't let us finish the game until he had hotels on every street and all the money in the bank.

Dad rented a television because he preferred getting it fixed and replaced for a monthly fee on a higher purchase rather than paying a big sum in one go. I realised recently that I was doing the same thing when I paid for a carpet to be laid. It was easier to pay monthly amounts rather than a big amount up front.

One thing Dad loved was gadgets and he got us what must have been one of the first video games that hooked up to our TV. There were a lot of wires. It played electronic ping-pong. The 'ball' went from one side of the screen to the other and the controls enabled you to move the 'bat' up and down. At the time it was so cool. I think most children now would laugh their heads off at such a slow and ridiculous game.

One day my dad gave me the most wonderful surprise for my birthday. We went on a plane from London to Edinburgh. I was allowed to go into the cockpit to speak to the pilot and it was so cool.

One thing I loved doing on my own was spinning around in circles. I would spin and spin until I fell over. I loved the feeling in my head of being giddy. Later I found out that in one spiritual tradition, the Sufis, actually do spinning to go into a spiritual trance; the Whirling Dervishes. I love to watch these on YouTube and hope to see them in real life one day.

Reflection:

As I reflect on my childhood I can see just how special my parents were.

Resources:

- *Sufi's Whirling Dervishes*: <u>youtu.be/ hkuimX1bh6g?feature=shared</u>
- Electronic Ping Pong - feel the thrill: <u>youtu.be/ fhd7FfGCdCo?feature=shared</u>

Chapter 7

Surviving School Plays, Piano and Tap Dancing Lessons!

"Be glad you don't live under me."
**Practising tap dancer lives in a flat / apartment
over someone else**

When I was in Primary School, I was in a play called *The Pirates Hat*. I remember that although I was the main character with a pirate's hat as you might expect, I also had to wear a dress at some point. Goodness only knows why.

Mum was hopeful that I would be the musical one in the family. I took Piano lessons for years and years. I didn't like it, but I didn't want to upset my mum. Much money was spent on all the lessons but even after years of lessons, I couldn't even read music. I somehow got to Grade 3 or 4 and although I could play a piece I memorised, I could only play a few pieces. One piece was *English Country Gardens* which my brother pointed out to me I wasn't playing correctly.

I also went to tap dancing classes. I was aware that it was girls who did the classes except for me, and many of them also did ballet classes. I think I would have enjoyed ballet but I felt uncomfortable that it wasn't a thing boys did so I stuck with tap dancing. I got the shoes and did it for a while, but left when I could do so.

When I was at boys' camp, I remember smuggling in a dress at the talent competition. I dressed up in the dress and sang silly songs. I can't remember it in great detail but I loved shocking the camp leaders and making the other boys laugh. It was a safer place than the school to be myself. I never subsequently had the desire to wear women's clothing but it was an experience I will never forget.

I will also not forget the boy's camp when we were playing the *wide game.* This is when two teams have to get a flag and take it to a location. But they have to deal with the opposing team who could take the flag from them. I don't know exactly what happened except that a whole group of lads landed on top of me and I felt my arm suddenly become very painful. When the game was over I told the leaders but they thought I was exaggerating. It wasn't until the next day that they decided they needed to take another boy to the Accident and Emergency because he had a tummy ache so they decided to take me as well. I was X-rayed and they found a greenstick fracture in my arm. The other boy, meanwhile, didn't have anything wrong apart from, except perhaps, homesickness!

One thing I loved was the Wednesday Rally. It was kind of a mid-week Sunday school and there were badges and sweets for learning bible verses and bible stories. When I was getting a bit older I asked if I could teach one evening, so I taught on 'Metamorphosis' and borrowed a Butterfly from my Biology class. I talked about how when we become

Christians we need to change and become something better.

Our church also had a reputation for organising amazing holidays. They converted an old ambulance and went to help some missionaries in Portugal. Then later they got a double-decker bus and started to travel throughout Europe on it. They organised a family trip my family went on where the adults were downstairs and the kids were upstairs. It was great fun and we saw the sites but my favourite part was when we went down the Hallstatt salt mines in Austria. You had to go down really long slides. It was so much fun. At one point the bus broke down far away from anything but when the leader went down the road they found a hostel with just the right number of beds. It felt like a miracle and we were so grateful. It certainly helped me develop my love of travelling.

Reflection:

Wearing dresses didn't mean I wanted to be a girl or a transgender. I think we need to be careful that we don't encourage children to be something when they are just having fun. However, today children are encouraged not to stick to stereotypical gender roles which I think is great.

Resource:

- See the *Hallstatt* salt mine extra long slides: youtu.be/xwu2y-1HybM?feature=shared

Chapter 8

Surviving Puberty

"When it comes to age, I just feel like puberty is, like, the most horrible time of anyone's life."
Sam Smith

Unfortunately when I was around eleven years old, I was diagnosed with an undescended testicle. I had wondered why I only seemed to have one and so was taken to the consultant. He was a classic consultant with no bedside manner and pushed me around like I was a sack of potatoes. He decided I did need surgery and I was in hospital for a few days. I was impressed with the kindness of the nurses.

I was less impressed by the children at school finding out and singing "Glenn Miles has only got one ball. The other is in the Albert Hall..." replacing Hitler's name with mine.

We had an extension built on the side of the house and two builders were working on it for several months. I was fascinated when they took their shirts off and showed their muscular frame. I used to sneak a peek out of the window but fortunately, I don't think they noticed me.

My older sister (8 years older than me) got engaged to a guy, John, who rode a motorbike. He was very masculine and I was very impressed with his deep voice. Occasionally he took me on the back of his motorbike to get something. I loved the smell of his leather jacket and the wind on my face and in my hair as we rode around. I felt so cool.

Also at this time my psoriasis, a chronic skin condition became visible on my elbows and scalp. It was related to stress. My nana also had it. She would say her patch was the size of a half crown. She insisted that hers was worse than mine! One day my brother and I went to Nana to watch a film called *'Stand Up Virgin Soldiers'*. We didn't talk about it but I think we were hoping it was more pornographic, but it was really about rookie soldiers. Nevertheless, a nosey neighbour told Nana what we were watching and Nana told Mum and then we were in trouble.

Down the road from Nana's house was a wooded area. I decided I needed to learn how to look cool smoking ciga-rettes so I bought a pack of ten and smoked them one after the other. I couldn't take any home because I was afraid I would get caught. But I was coughing and retching and threw up. As a result, I never smoked tobacco again!

One time my mother talked with me about gay people. She said that it was a very difficult thing for those who had that label. I realise now it wasn't disapproval but just recog-nition that it was a difficult lifestyle but at the time I felt she was saying it was wrong and aligning with what I felt from the church.

One time in the physical education school changing rooms, just as puberty hit, I somehow developed an erection. Some of the boys saw this and started laughing at me. I didn't know how to handle their laughter. I was so embarrassed and I told them to stop laughing at me which, of course, made it even worse. When they asked me why I had an erection, I told them I thought it must be because everyone was staring at me. I didn't even realise at the time that it was probably because I had seen the boys who had already gone through puberty in the showers.

As I got older, I realised that I didn't have much interest in girls in the same way that the other boys did. The few boys I hung around with were not very masculine themselves and didn't enjoy doing masculine pursuits including developing relationships with girls. We didn't talk about that kind of stuff but occasionally one of the other boys would talk to me in the lunch queue and question why I was the way that I was. They, of course, would exaggerate their apparent 'conquests' with girls and ask me why I didn't have the same interests. I honestly didn't know.

I independently chose to become a born-again Christian when I was a young teenager. As a Christian boy, I believed that God loved me and many stories in The Bible impressed me. I loved the stories of Jesus and his parables but I loved reading how David and Jonathan had such a close relationship 'greater than the love of a woman' and I longed for that kind of deep close friendship myself. When I was sixteen I decided to be baptised alongside other young men my age. It was a public statement that I was a Christian and felt very significant. I didn't feel pressured in any way. It was my choice.

I was confused when I read the story of Esau and Jacob about a boy who appeared to be favoured not only by his father but also God. I wrongly read into it that God preferred masculine men and less of those who were in any way effeminate. What I considered was a high-pitched effeminate voice (it really wasn't!) seemed to exclude me.

I started collecting cacti and succulents. So many different kinds. My dad built me shelves on the windows in the extension room at the back of the house. I would help out a local cactus fanatic who had a huge greenhouse and he would give me cacti every month or so as a way of thanking him. I became a local member of the *British Cactus and Succulent Society* and won several prizes for showing my cacti. I know, very nerdy.

A friendly guy my age, also called Steve (M) who later became a photographer, offered to photograph my cacti and I used them to illustrate my project for Biology 'O' level. I know, very nerdy indeed! My dad put shelves up in the conservatory for me to show off my cacti and also made me a wormery, two flat pieces of glass with earth in between where I could keep worms. It was typical of his practical way of fathering.

One thing I didn't have to deal with as a teenager was online exploitation. Boys between 14-18 years are currently at the highest risk of sexploitation (more than 90% of cases) where an online friendship turns out to be grooming which can lead to blackmail and extortion. Teachers and parents of boys this age need to be aware of this and help educate children on the dangers.

Reflection:

I think that encouraging children to do hobbies is very important. Sport was not something I enjoyed, but clubs and hobbies I adored.

Resources:

- *The National Hamster Association UK*: britishhamsterassociation.org.uk/about.php
- *The British Cactus and Succulent Society*: bcss.org.uk
- The best age of surgery for undescended testes: nejm.org/doi/full/10.1056/NEJMoa067588
- Helping Protect Children from Sexploitation - *Internet Watch Foundation*: iwf.org.uk

Or scan me instead!

Chapter 9

Surviving a Near-Shipwreck

"God protected Paul when he was in a boat when the ship was shipwrecked."
Acts 27:1 - 28:16

One time, aged around 14 years old, I went on holiday with big (as opposed to little) Steve P and we stayed with his older brother in Penzance, Cornwall. They had porn magazines in piles around the house. It was such a contrast to what I was used to with my church background. Of course, the porn was heterosexual. I was so conflicted. I wanted to look but I couldn't because I was a Christian. But when I did glance over to what my friend was looking at I wasn't at all impressed by what I saw. It just seemed gross.

We wanted to go to the Scilly Isles so we decided to get the boat over there from the mainland. I think if it had been when this book was written the health and safety regulations, and even the Coast Guard, would have stopped boats from going due to a big storm happening. It was raining from the moment we woke up until we got home. We got to the boat just at the last minute. We weren't late but later we wished we had been! We didn't even consider not to go.

The voyage also was supposed to give us a stunning seaside view of Cornwall's quaint villages and the Land's End peninsula but it was so cloudy we couldn't see anything apart from steep waves. I was hoping we would be joined and followed by pods of dolphins, a raft of seabirds and even basking sharks but none of this happened!

It was terribly stormy and the boat was really just a small fishing boat. The boat you are on has a major impact on how seasick members of your party may feel. In general, the larger the boat, the less it rocks and the fewer people will feel seasick. This was a small fishing boat and we were certainly being tossed and turned around. Even those who were familiar with this route were being seasick over the side of the boat. Lots of people.

We weren't involved in a shipwreck of course, but as a teenager with the seasickness it certainly felt like we were unlikely to survive. It seemed to last forever but it was only a few hours. We finally arrived at the destination but the storm didn't stop and everything in the town seemed to be shut up. We found a bus stop with a roof and so we ended up sitting waiting for the storm to pass, and for the seasickness to pass. Just as we were starting to feel a bit better... then it was time to get back on the boat! We were relieved to be home.

Reflection:

OK so it wasn't a shipwreck but it didn't stop me being afraid that it could have been! I actually love travelling on all kinds of boats so it didn't put me off but I prefer not to travel on a fishing boat to the Scilly Isles again!

Resource:

- Modern boats to the Scilly Isles if you dare: visitislesofscilly.com/travel/by-sea

Chapter 10

Surviving Being Mugged in a Cathedral!

"It's better to get mugged than to live a life of fear."
Freeman Dyson

I enjoyed getting the train to London on my own as a teenager. One day I went with my friend also called Steve (B) and we visited the beautiful St. Paul's Cathedral. We went up into the whispering gallery which has a great view down into the Crypt. Three boys unexpectedly came up behind us, grabbed us around our necks and stole Steve's wallet and passport. I suppose I didn't have anything worth pinching. They ran off before we could do anything.

We tried to report it to the minister but they were too busy conducting an evensong service! I was disappointed with the Cathedral staff that they didn't take us seriously. I don't think they could have done anything but listening to us in a compassionate way might have helped. Perhaps echoes of the future.

Jesus deeply impressed me. The way he was compassionate and gentle and yet strong made him a great role model. I was drawn to caring for things - plants, animals, and people. I worked in a horticultural nursery during the school holidays and weekends. I visited my nanna and great auntie Ivy regularly and volunteered at the local hospital for people with learning difficulties, learning and then teaching MAKATON (a simple deaf language) to deaf people with learning difficulties.

When I was sixteen I got a job in a Marie Curie home as a nursing assistant on Saturdays. Some people told my parents that they thought it was odd that a young man would want to do that but I loved caring for people, even though they were dying. I remember my first patient who was blind and we got on well. I was sad when he died but understood this would not be the last death I would see.

I grew up in a church that was very good with young people. The Sunday school teachers and youth leaders were all committed to ensuring that we were well-versed in scripture and we were encouraged to learn and memorise bible verses. All the leaders in the church were strong believers in the purity movement and we were encouraged to 'behave' which meant no sexual behaviour until marriage.

My dad was in the travel industry and was a founding member of *'The Gangplank'* an organisation of men in the industry who wanted to help children by buying equipment and running charitable events to raise funds. It was an honourable thing to do and they helped many children's organisations. One of the organisations was the local authority children's home where there were children mainly from Lambeth who were taken away from their families by social services for various reasons. This deeply impacted me.

Dad used to visit the orphanage to determine their needs and see if the *Gangplank* could help. On one such occasion, he saw who is now my sister Binnie who was just 10 days old at the time and afterwards went home and spoke to my mum about whether they should seek to adopt her. We visited her regularly. I was very fond of her and two years later after all the paperwork had been completed she came to live with us.

Reflection:

Although getting mugged was a horrible experience it didn't put Steve B off as he is now a Bishop himself! I do think it was a symbolic representation of how the church gets focused on itself and forgets the importance of real people.

Resource:

- St. Paul's Cathedral but take protection! (not a knife or guns though!): stpauls.co.uk

Chapter 11

Surviving Sexual Curiosity and Shame

*"Shame is the most powerful, master emotion. It's the fear
that we're not good enough."*
Brene Brown

I felt so deeply ashamed that I even felt attracted to
boys and this was encouraged by what I was being
taught in the church. It affected my friendships with
boys because I was afraid to get too close to them. My two
friends Steve P. and I were the boys who hated sports and
were close to our mums. In retrospect, it is fascinating that
other boys sensed the difference we were and called us 'gay'
even before we realised it. All three of us later came out as
gay. Had we been conditioned by this teasing or was it
something deeper than that?

There was a boys camp that I was encouraged to go to
every year by my church and it was run by a local Christian
group that worked hard to make it fun for all the boys and
teach us about the Bible. I was excited when one of the boys

touched me on the leg and it was clear what his intentions were. We found a quiet place and touched each other and it felt good. Nothing more was said about it and I went home. But again, later I was deeply ashamed.

I had similar experiences with other boys during my early teenage years but I wouldn't even consider having a relationship of any depth with another boy at that time. It just wasn't acceptable in the church environment in which I lived, but I longed for a deeper friendship with a boy of the same age.

Pre-online shopping it was possible to order things from a large bulky catalogue and pay back over time. My mum had two of these sent every few months and she saved them to press flowers. When everyone was out of the house I used to look through the catalogues for the men's underwear section to see men with big chests and muscles. I was not impressed a bit by the women's underwear section.

I worked in a garden centre at the weekends and holidays for a few years. In the staff tea room there were several tabloids with naked women on page 3. Occasionally they would have hunky shirtless men on page 8 (I assumed for the women?). I was entranced and would occasionally tear that page out when no one was around to take it home. One time my mum saw something when I was emptying my pockets and told me to throw it in the dustbin. I was excruciatingly embarrassed.

I didn't seem to have a problem when it came to friendships with girls. They interestingly considered me to be safe and I enjoyed their company. Sometimes other boys would get jealous that I could be so comfortable with other girls when they felt so awkward with them.

My parents didn't know what to do about sex education. My mum gave me a book to read on sex and told me to lock myself in their bedroom to read it. My dad never spoke to me about sex. I wanted him to but I assume he was embarrassed to do so. I really needed him to talk to me.

I borrowed a copy of a book called *"Confessions of a Window Cleaner"* from a friend. I barricaded myself in the toilet at home and tried to get 'turned on' by the heterosexual sex stories in the stories but I couldn't.

Reflection:

It's hard for parents and teachers to talk to children about sex, but it is important that they do so. Otherwise, they will learn wrong information from porn. In some ways I am grateful I was so naive about it. Children today don't have that luxury.

Resource:

- Talking to children about sex: <u>raisingchildren. net.au/pre-teens/development/puberty-sexual- development/sex-education</u>

Chapter 12

Surviving Child Sexual Abuse

"The sexual abuse and exploitation of children is one of the most vicious crimes conceivable, a violation of mankind's most basic duty to protect the innocent."
James T. Walsh

1 in 4 girls and 1 in 6 boys experience child sexual abuse.

Occasionally, as a child, I would go to Christian retreats/conferences that were open to people of all ages and denominations. I went to a conference centre in the south of England with my mum and it was in a beautiful house overlooking a lake. When we arrived we were encouraged to find rooms where we could sleep for the nights we were there and many of the rooms had different bed arrangements in them. The room I chose had just one bunk bed and I put my stuff in the bottom of the bunk bed and went off to join in the day's activities. When I came back to my room later there was a guy there probably in his 30s and he introduced himself and disappeared to do what he was planning to do. I didn't see him until much later when I was already in bed.

He casually talked to me as he undressed. He was happy to tell me about himself and he made me feel comfortable. As he took all his clothes off and unnecessarily removed them as he faced me, he didn't feel embarrassed about me seeing his body even though he was naked. I was very curious and couldn't take my eyes off him. He told me that he had worked as a chauffeur for Margaret Thatcher which impressed me and I got the impression he was a 'man about town'. He told me that he had had several girlfriends and made it clear that he was very sexually experienced.

He later asked me if I had ever seen a man naked before and I shyly responded that I had not (apart from him about ten minutes earlier). He invited me to take a look at him on the top bunk and I peered over the edge of the bed to see him fully erect. He assured me that he 'wasn't gay' and there was no need for me to be afraid. We were 'just two men doing what men did'.

It didn't take long before he was encouraging me to do more than just watch and over the next two days he sexually abused me. I felt guilty but I also felt excited. I think that if it had been only that physical experience then I could have gotten over it quickly, but it had a psychological and emotional impact it had on me over many years. In fact, it still impacts me after five decades.

I assumed that because my penis had been erect and I had chosen to look at him, then it was my fault. I assumed that I had been instrumental in making it happen. I assumed that I was the one at fault. I was deeply ashamed of myself. How could I do such a thing? I really got confused about what had happened. Was I now gay? Has he *made* me gay? The word scared me. So I just pushed it down and tried not to think about it. But I did think about it. A lot.

I blamed myself because I was intrigued to see a real man's naked body. I told myself for some time that I could have just rolled over and ignored him, but could I have?

Even though I had gone to the conference with my mother I couldn't tell her what happened to me, and I didn't dare to tell anyone. I doubt at that time the centre had child safeguarding policies but even if they had, I didn't dare to tell anyone so nothing could have been done.

For years I couldn't tell anyone. It wasn't until I was around 23 years old, ten years later, that I spoke to a youth leader in my church. He was genuinely concerned and said some kind words to me, but later he considered that this was what led me to be attracted to men. At that stage I didn't think we were able to do anything about the guy who abused me; I thought it was too late.

I have recently contacted the retreat centre and checked on their child safeguarding policy, and the Christian organisation that was holding the retreat, and was glad to see that they have made policy changes.

Reflection:

In retrospect, I believe that my experience of sexual abuse was not what caused me to be gay. I was already predisposed to that. But it was deeply wrong of him to take advantage of a boy who was still going through puberty. He had no idea how it would still haunt me 50 years later. I also now realise that I was totally not at fault.

Resources:

- *"It's Not My Fault"* by Lamont Hiebert: <u>youtu.be/lHTHwIb447M?feature=shared</u>
- Sexual abuse of boys and men: <u>rainn.org/articles/sexual-assault-men-and-boys</u>
- Research evidence of sexual abuse of boys: <u>1in6.org</u>

Or scan me instead!

Chapter 13

Surviving Hiking on a Glacier in Norway

"A glacier will frequently move forward one foot while retreating three feet... Which reminds me a lot of myself!"
Charles M. Schulz

When I was eighteen I travelled to America to work in a church of the Brethren camp under 'Camp America'. As I left for the airport my mother explained to my dad that I was "leaving as a boy and would return as a man". It felt very significant to me. I loved experiencing a new culture and working with children. The camp mostly had one-week camps for children from poor urban cities on the Eastern seaboard and was based in Pennsylvania. I learned new skills including caring for homesick children. At night I was responsible for eight to ten children in a log cabin, sleeping alongside them in the cabin. I'm sure modern child protection professionals would not have agreed but it was what it was at that time. Most nights I just slept and there were no problems. The kids loved it and many didn't want to go home.

We didn't get much time off but when we did we headed into *Penn State*, the main University city which was a few hours' drive from the very rural location the camp was in. One weekend we went to see the *'Rocky Horror Picture Show'*. Our team of 'camp counsellors' didn't do so but many people dressed up. I had never seen a transvestite before and I didn't know whether to feel horrified or excited. After I finished camp counselling I met up with some of the other staff and later visited Niagara Falls on a *Greyhound* bus. It was amazing.

The church I belonged to had a very active youth group and in many ways, it was a safe place for me. They organised many activities including vacations overseas. I was close to several young women because of my fear of getting too close to a young man. I was afraid that if I got into a loving relationship it might become homosexual. These holidays provided a contrast to the 'sun, sea and sex' of the 18 to 30s holidays, which were actively being promoted in the eighties, with 'sun, sea and *scripture*' regular evening bible studies. Many Christian couples met on these holidays including my brother Nick and his wife Fiona. Any gay relationships would have been completely unacceptable.

But I enjoyed the skiing holidays and actually did better than I expected. I started in the Black Forest in Germany and progressed to Austria and Grindelwald in Switzerland. I loved the feel of skiing down slopes and enjoying apre-ski juggertea and gluwein.

One time we went to hike on a glacier in Norway. It was an incredible experience being roped to each other and peering down into the depths of deep crevices. Glacier Hiking has become a tourist attraction in some countries, but it requires special knowledge of the constantly changing environments and glacial features. Hazards like crevasses and serac (ice columns) are difficult obstacles that glacier hikers should be aware of during this activity.

Snow bridges may conceal deep crevasses on glaciers or hidden cavities under snowfields. These bridges may collapse under the weight of an unsuspecting hiker. We were tied together with a rope but in retrospect, I wonder whether the guides were as qualified as they appeared. With global warming, I imagine it is even more dangerous than before.

Although I loved being part of the church, in retrospect I feel it continued to have an over-emphasis on sin which left me always feeling not good enough. I think this draws a lot of gay children away from many churches, or traps them in a context where they feel they can never be fully what God intended them to be.

Reflection:

One thing you learn from hiking on a glacier is that you are tied together and totally depend on each other. It is a reminder that you can't handle a danger/challenge alone.

Resource:

- The best hiking glaciers in Norway: <u>muchbetteradventures.com/magazine/norways-most-stunning-glacier-hikes</u>

Chapter 14

Surviving Teenage and early Twenties

"When you are in your teenage years you are consciously experiencing everything for the first time, so adolescent stories are all beginnings. There are never any endings."
Aidan Chambers

When I was 16 years I went to a technical college to do my A levels, Biology and Sociology. I only managed to pass one - Sociology - which I enjoyed doing. I loved plants and animals but Biology A level was so boring. In my summer holiday, I did a research project with other young people on a bus travelling to Europe. It was called *'The Interaction of Young People in a Closed Environment'*. My sociology teacher loved it. I enjoyed technical college much more than secondary school where I was finally free from bullying.

My favourite day was during 'rag week' when I dressed up as a punk rocker. I did the makeup and everything! On my way home I got on the bus and a lady dropped her glove so I instinctively picked it up for her. She thanked me but appeared confused as it seemed to conflict with my persona. When I got back to the town I lived in I deliberately hung out near the secondary school I had grown up in. The students were shocked to see me, Glenn Miles, the punk rocker! It just seemed too incredulous to be true. When I got home my father had a friend visit. He insisted that I open the door in all my gear to tease his friend. What a fun day to remember!

When I was nineteen, I worked in a huge hospital for people with severe learning difficulties/mental illnesses when it was still a Victorian asylum in architecture. It was before they developed community programs. I was a porter and worked with a group of other guys who transported food and supplies around the hospital in electric carts. It was great fun seeing how many joined-up carts we could get around the corners! I did this for a few months. It wasn't always easy. Delivering trollies to some of the locked wards you could hear what sounded like people screaming in distress. It did make me question how God could allow people to be in so much emotional pain.

While some of my peers were starting to go on dates, I did try to go out with someone. I remember getting dressed up in my velvet trousers. However, she didn't turn up and I was kind of relieved because I didn't really like her. In my head, I was still struggling with same-sex attraction. I understand that age 19 in young men is the time their sexuality is at its peak. I felt that my sexual feelings were above and beyond what was normal but how would I know when I didn't talk about sex with anyone?

My fears of being gay led me to think that being gay was wrong and that I needed to be punished for it. So every time something went wrong I would believe it was my fault for being gay.

Meanwhile, the church that I grew up in encouraged romantic, but non-sexual, relationships between boys and girls, but not boys and boys or girls and girls. I continued to believe that it was wrong and safer not to get into an emotional relationship with another young man so I mostly avoided them, and my friends were mainly young women.

I have recently done research for the *Matt & Naz Foundation* which found that 32% of youth participants most frequently reported their parents/caregivers initially responded to their 'coming out' with grief and sadness. This can split families.

There was one story in the hospital where I worked where one of the porter staff had sex with a patient in a cleaner's cupboard. He thought he would get away with it but she identified him and he thankfully was prosecuted for it.

Reflection:

It is sad in retrospect that as a young gay man, I felt I ought to date a girl rather than a boy, but the culture, particularly the church culture, wouldn't allow such a thing.

Resources:

- *First Light*: Making a referral for church-related abuse: firstlight.org.uk/make-a-referral

Or scan me instead!

- *Matt & Naz Foundation* is a charity that helps parents from conservative faith backgrounds who have children who 'come out' who need help trying to come to terms with it: nazandmattfoundation.org

Chapter 15

Surviving 'Heaven'

"Heaven grant us patience with a man in love."
Rudyard Kipling

Burrswood was a beautiful healing centre in Kent. People would go there to different services where they could be prayed for. They could come for the day or stay in a respite building where they would receive nursing care, or another building as a retreat. Before I started my nursing training, I worked as a nursing assistant. People were able to work there who would have found it difficult to work anywhere else because they were accepted and had a role. I was deeply impressed. Some places seem to be closer to heaven than others. This was one such place. Sadly it recently closed due to insufficient funding.

Dorothy, the person who started the centre, had experienced a miraculous healing at the point of dying. She believed she met Jesus and was asked if she wanted to go back. She said she sensed that God had a plan for her to set up a healing ministry. I have subsequently heard of this happening with a number of people that are close to death. The choice of heaven or returning to earth must be a difficult choice when you see the reality of heaven.

Although the majority of those who came did not receive dramatic healing, everyone who came seemed to leave in a better state than when they arrived. It was a good lesson in including spiritual care in the holistic care of people. Sometimes I would sit in the chapel and talk to God about 'my predicament'. I wanted to 'pray the gay away'. One of the older women who worked there seemed to understand my challenge. She couldn't talk about it with me, but I had a sense she understood and was praying for me.

There was a guy who I got talking to, one of the staff, Bernard, who had previously been a monk. He told me about the monastery he had previously lived in and that he had decided, because of his sexuality, that he could not continue to be there. I later met up with him in London. He seemed to be attracted to me but he didn't push it and we just remained friends.

I later visited the monastery and loved being in such a beautiful place dedicated to God. They grew tomatoes. It was a silent order and every day when they had visitors they would meet with them to talk for an hour. This was a different way of being a man and I liked it.

One time, however, Bernard and I went to visit *'Heaven'*, a popular gay club in London. It was a fascinating experience for me to be in an environment where it was OK to be gay. There were some beautiful men and some seemed attracted to me but ultimately I felt it was wrong, so I never went back. I know some who would have described it more as hell than heaven. One friend was appalled that I even went to it saying it was likely to tempt me to "go off the rails".

Later, I lived not far from the *'Vauxhall Tavern',* one of the most well-known gay pubs in South London. I was too nervous to go into it but one day when I came home very late from going out with friends I decided to go to see what was going on. It was around 2.30 am. It was a big show night and I could see around the door that there were men with their shirts off. As I went to the door a bouncer asked me what I was doing. I said I wanted to come in. He said I couldn't. I don't really know why but I have the feeling to this day that it was the right thing for me at that time. I was young and naive and I think he realised I was far too vulnerable at the time. I never went back.

As I have got older I consider the many incredibly vulnerable people I have worked with who are experiencing hell now. I cannot believe that they will experience hell when they die as well. I believe that God's grace will draw them to Himself.

Reflection:

I believe that our current experiences on earth are preparing us for a new heaven and a new earth. Then everything will be as it should be.

Resources:

- *"We are looking forward to a new heaven and a new earth, where righteousness dwells"* (**2 Peter 3:13 NIV**).
- *"And God shall wipe away all tears from their eyes and there shall be no more death, neither sorrow, nor crying, neither shall there be any pain for the former things are passed away"* (**Revelation 21:4 The Message**).

Chapter 16

Surviving Sex Discrimination

"We pledge ourselves to liberate all our people from the continuing bondage of poverty, deprivation, suffering, gender and other discrimination."
Nelson Mandela

I n March 1980, aged 19 years, I became a student nurse at St. Thomas Hospital in London. The day I arrived I was taken to my room in the nurse's home and my breath was taken away because there was an incredible view of the Houses of Parliament outside my bedroom window. I was one of four men in a group of sixty (the rest all being women!). One of the guys described himself as a communist, the other already had training as a psychiatric nurse and came over as having mental illness himself and the last guy described himself as gay. He collected Victorian snuff boxes and had silk scarves. None of us got on with each other but the first night the gay guy was determined to show me the real Soho. We walked over Westminster

Bridge and I loved seeing all the bright lights of the city. We got as far as Leicester Square but when we got to the red light area I felt uncomfortable, so I turned around and went home. He described me as a 'sweet boy' but we never went out after that or had anything much to do with each other. I made friends with a group of female nurses in the flat next door and I stayed friends with them throughout the course and beyond.

After the 'feminisation of nursing' in the 19th century, it became socially inappropriate for males to provide intimate care for female patients. It was also theorised that men were not fit for nursing because the rough hands of men were *"not fitted to touch, bathe and dress wounded limbs"*. Some people still view that male nurses do not conform to the traditional gender-stereotyped role that women are the care-takers, and many consider nursing to be a women-only profession. (*Wikipedia* 2024)

Being a male nurse was a mixed blessing for the ward sister. As so few male nurses worked in general nursing as opposed to mental health they still didn't quite know what to do with me. Should I work with women? Most women didn't seem to mind at all and I always asked them if they were comfortable with me helping them in the more intimate tasks. If they said they were not comfortable I would ask a female nurse to help. I doubted the female nurses asked the male patients the same question, even if I was present. If there was a heavy patient, I would always be asked to help to lift them up the bed. Some hoists were available to lift people into the bath but these were not used to the extent that they are used nowadays. I still have the backache to prove it!

Mostly, medical students didn't mix with male nurses. I could see them sometimes pointing at me and hear them gossiping about whether I was gay or not. But most of the time they ignored me. I didn't have the confidence to try to build relationships with them and none of them made the effort to connect with me as a student nurse. Later I had the opportunity to share a house with a group of medical students. One of them, Dom, was incredibly encouraging and supportive. He was an exceptional man.

In the midwifery unit, the midwife trainer made it quite clear that she wasn't happy about me working there but she had no choice. It was part of my training.

In spite of this, I really enjoyed my overall nurse training. It helped my confidence in supporting people in difficult circumstances. People sometimes say that men should experience the discipline of the armed forces but I would suggest that nurse training teaches a much wider range of skills from birth to death. I worked in a newborn unit, assisted midwives, worked in an operating theatre, worked in an Accident and Emergency, worked in an iron lung unit, managed a renal ward, and my favourite was working with children in the paediatric unit.

When people asked me what I did I obviously would say I was a nurse. People were often surprised and the response was 'What a male nurse?' I would respond by saying that I was the last time I checked!

During my nurse training, we all worked very hard. We worked on the wards and then this was interspersed with 'academic' training in the nursing school. By the end of the training, we could manage a ward. But one time we had a four-week holiday. Many of my colleagues took the opportunity to go skiing but I chose to go to India.

I never, of course, experienced racism but my adopted daughter from Cambodia has done and it always breaks my heart to hear about it. Her first day in her new secondary school she was slammed against the wall by someone. As a young mother, she was in a shopping area and a group of juveniles told her to go back to where she came from. When she was working as a waitress a group got up and backed away when she took them their food because they were afraid she was from China and had personally brought COVID with her! Of course these are just a few examples and I know she has a lot more, but that's her story.

Reflection:

I know that sex discrimination against women is far more prevalent than against women but all discrimination is unnecessary, unhelpful and unkind.

Resource:

- Sex discrimination against men in the workplace: <u>personneltoday.com/hr/sex-discrimination-against-men-10-ways</u>

Or scan me instead!

Chapter 17

Surviving Conversion Therapy

"Historically, conversion therapy was intended to change homosexuals' sexual orientation and turn them 'straight'. Harsh methods such as electric shock therapy and chemical castration were used. More recently, talking therapies became the usual mode of delivery, mainly by religious groups, and it was also said to have been offered to those who were or thought they might be transgender. There is no evidence that it works."

British Medical Journal April 2022

I t is hard to explain to some young people today the challenges of growing up in an environment where it was just *wrong* to be gay. It was very subtle but the message was clear. What this meant for me was that I needed to avoid getting into relationships with men that were in any way deep, for fear that it could become emotional or, worse still, sexual. So I felt safer having friendships with women and they seemed to feel safe with me.

In a heteronormative culture, all relationships portrayed on TV and in the cinema were between males and females. I longed to see men with their shirts off. I loved watching The *Six Million Dollar Man* and the 'bromance' of *Starsky and Hutch*. I got a tan leather jacket like 'Hutch' and I was so proud of it.

I also loved watching the TV mini-series *'The Thorn Birds'* starring Richard Chamberlain. He was so handsome and I longed for someone to love and hold me like that

My sexual feelings towards men continued and I discovered porn magazines. I found one in a rubbish bin and then I started to occasionally purchase them. Buying them was excruciatingly uncomfortable, very different from the anonymous access online for most young people today but I think it stopped me from it becoming too much of a regular habit.

Porn had many negative side effects including making me feel that my body was inadequate. Occasionally, I wanted to meet other men and I learnt the signals gay men used to connect. But it all just left me feeling a pathetic loser and I hated myself even more. I would go home and cry in my room and curse myself for being such a pervert.

I did talk to Dave, my youth pastor about what had happened to me and he was kind and supportive. He encouraged me to keep closely in touch with him and to keep him informed. It really helped. I know that for many of my gay peers, these kinds of conversations ended in a disaster where they might be excommunicated from the church or publicly humiliated.

At around the same time, I found an advertisement in a

Christian magazine which offered counselling for Christian men in London with 'same-sex attraction'. I contacted them of my own volition hoping that I could find someone to help me convert my feelings to become straight. It couldn't. The counsellor invited me to sit on his lap which I chose to do. He had a strong aftershave. But it was confusing and felt uncomfortable. Even though he asked if I was Ok to sit on his lap, I was too afraid to tell him "Not really".

I started going to Christian retreats for men who believed that same-sex attraction could only be resolved by remaining celibate or being 'healed' and then being able to marry a woman. It was nice to connect to other men and some seemed happy in their chosen lifestyle but some seemed as confused as me.

I worried, "Was I going to abuse children because I myself was abused?" If I admitted I am gay would it prevent me from working with children even though I never felt sexually attracted to children?

In recent years I have made contact with Jeremy who ran one of the organisations that were previously involved in encouraging men with same-sex attractions to change their behaviour. Jeremy changed his theological under-standing of what was right and began to believe that it was OK to be Christian and gay. Sadly, he experienced the consequences. He has since become married to a man and provides a different kind of support to Christian men who are gay.

I also believe that maintaining a milieu that 'being gay is wrong' which most churches continue to do, is as effective in its negativity as actual counselling men and boys to not be gay. The church I grew up in still feels that it is wrong for the church to 'compromise their beliefs' to accommodate modern LGBTQ cultural beliefs. However, I think the reality is that LGBTQ are still not widely accepted in society and most churches don't want to make the brave decision to accept LGBTQ people which could cause some people to leave the church. They do not consider how they themselves are alienating a whole community of people.

Reflection:

The different parts of the body are all needed so if the church is rejecting the LGBTQ community what are they also rejecting? Perhaps they are rejecting those who could contribute to, for example, the artistic and pastoral aspects of the community?

21 *The eye can't say to the hand, "I don't need you!" The head can't say to the feet, "I don't need you!"*
22 *In fact, it is just the opposite. The parts of the body that seem to be weaker are the ones we can't do without.*
23 *The parts that we think are less important we treat with special honour. The private parts aren't shown. But they are treated with special care.*
24 *The parts that can be shown don't need special care. But God has put together all the parts of the body. And he has given more honour to the parts that didn't have any.*
25 *In that way, the parts of the body will not take sides. All of them will take care of one another.*
26 *If one part suffers, every part suffers with it. If one part is honoured, every part shares in its joy.*
27 *You are the body of Christ. Each one of you is a part of it.*
1 Corinthians 12: 21-27

Resources:

- *The Trevor Project*: Resources for Supporting Survivors of Conversion Therapy & thetrevorproject.org

Glenn Miles PhD

Or scan me instead!

Chapter 18

Surviving the HIV 'bullet'

The estimated 630 000 [480 000–880 000] people dying from HIV globally in 2022 were 69% fewer than in 2004 (the peak)
World Health Organisation (2024)

I am very aware that the late Eighties and Nineties were one of the peak times when people were vulnerable to getting HIV. As a nurse, I knew something about the prevention side but I was too embarrassed to get the erotic leaflets used to educate young gay men. What if someone found them? There was not the medication that there is now. So many men my age were getting and dying of AIDs. The British Government's public health 'tombstone' campaign in the UK was deliberately designed to create fear in an attempt to change behaviour. But it marginalised gay men even more.

I continued to believe that it was wrong for me to have any emotional engagement with other men. If I started to get emotionally attached to someone I would back off and hide myself away. I spent too much time in church environments which was a bubble away from the real world, so I was very naive.

However, I did discover that certain public bathrooms were a meet-up for gay men, known as cottaging. In retrospect, I am surprised I wasn't harmed. I was certainly deeply ashamed and thought I could never be forgiven for being so perverse.

I was impressed that *Mildmay Mission Hospital* had changed its focus from tropical medicine to helping young men who were dying of HIV in a non-judgemental way, despite the messages of some in the church which suggested that HIV was God's punishment for people with HIV

I realise that this could have ended very differently for me if I had been raped or succumbed to someone with HIV who was not adequately protected. I was afraid to buy or carry condoms with me.

Later, in Cambodia, I supported the development of the *HALO* (Help and Love for Orphans) programme for children orphaned because of HIV. It became a model for local foster care started by my friends Craig and Nay.

At the same time, Siobhan worked for *Maryknoll,* a Catholic organisation that provided health care for people who had acquired HIV.

When we returned to the UK, she became the HIV nurse practitioner for the Swansea area. I know she was much loved by patients and staff but I think it was also very hard for her emotionally and she did not receive the counselling support that such a position deserved.

Reflection:

I am aware that in different circumstances I might have had a risky lifestyle that led to AIDs. I was spared this from happening, but I know it could have been very different.

Resource:

- HIV/AIDs in the UK: <u>nhs.uk/conditions/hiv-and-aids</u>

Chapter 19

Surviving Falling down a Hole in India

"The rabbit-hole went straight on like a tunnel for some way and then dipped suddenly down, so suddenly that Alice had not a moment to think about stopping herself before she found herself falling down a very deep well."
Alice in Wonderland, Lewis Carroll 1865

Whilst many of my colleagues in the Nightingale School of Nursing went skiing in Europe I chose to go to work in a *Salvation Army* hospital in Southern India whilst my friend Julie, who was also a student nurse, worked with the *Salvation Army* in Sri Lanka.

When I was in Sri Lanka I visited the *British Club*. It had a swimming pool in the shape of British India with Sri Lanka being the children's pool. It was a reminder of a different era. In the changing room, two absolutely beautiful men were changing. It was the first time I had seen real men naked (apart from my abuser) and I was gobsmacked. I'm glad they didn't notice me because my mouth dropped open as if I was frozen in time and I had an erection.

My main purpose was to work in South India with the S*alvation Army.* This was before it became common for people to do mission trips and I had to organise it all myself. I was deeply impressed by the way the Sally (Salvation) Army had worked in this hospital for over a hundred years. I have always been impressed with their attitude to social justice and their commitment to the poorest. Most of the staff were locals with just a few missionaries left involved in training locals.

I remember getting off the aeroplane in Trivandrum India and being overcome by the sheer volume of the crowds of people in the street. This wasn't the last time I was moved by the volume of people in India. I remember thinking it was like everyone had just come out of the cinema, but all the time.

It took me a while to get used to the humidity. I was treated as a student nurse and worked alongside other student nurses there. It was a great experience. I helped care for one man who had an infected wound that was effectively treated with maggots. I was also invited to help with a caesarean section performed under local anaesthetic because the anaesthetist was off that day! However, because I was tall and long-armed, my arms kept falling out of the sleeves of the Asian size scrubs exposing my wrists which were 'unclean', so I had to stop.

On my days off I cycled through the fascinating local tropical villages and got the bus to the southern tip of India. I loved being outside in the monsoonal rains. The local children were fascinated with the white man and surrounded me in a circle to watch me as I sat on the beach. I dipped my feet in but learned not to swim in the sea from the children who kept their distance from it.

A couple of young men took me out one evening and we were walking along the path. As we were walking I suddenly fell into a hole. Everyone else apparently knew to avoid that particular spot but as this was my first time in that particular area, I had fallen in it. It was about up to my waist. They pulled me out and I realised that I was lucky not to have broken anything though I did twist my ankle. I was pretty bruised up and they had to pull me out and take me home. I managed it with my arms around the two guy's shoulders.

As I left India I felt sure that I would return to India. After I completed my obligation in the hospital and earned my silver enamel 'Nightingale' badge for graduating from St.Thomas Hospital, I returned to work in another Sally Army hospital in Maharashtra. Once again I was impressed and felt that the medical mission was my "calling".

The Salvation Army are now one of the key organisations addressing modern-day slavery/human trafficking in the world. I continue to be impressed with the way they balance outreach in word and deed.

After I finished the work part of my trip I met up with my friend Julie and we had a wonderful trip around north India visiting Delhi, Jaipur, Udaipur and of course the Taj Mahal but the day we went to see this spectacular building we had previously been staying at a hostel with bedbugs. Of course, me being sensitive and allergic to their bites, my back was covered in large angry red uncomfortable welts!

Reflection:

Going to India was like falling down the rabbit hole into a completely new world. It was exciting to find myself in such a different place. One friend at home teased me that I liked it to enjoy the adulation of being the white man but it wasn't how I saw it. I loved the sense of adventure and learning. I somehow knew this was to be my future, my calling.

Resources:

- *Salvation Army* information on their approach to Modern Slavery: salvationarmy.org.uk/modern-slavery & salvationarmy.org.uk/modern-slavery/modern-slavery-latest-reports

Chapter 20

Surviving the Freezing Arctic

"The Arctic Circle at approximately 66°30' N. marks the southern limit of the area within which, for one day or more each year, the sun does not set (about June 21) or rise (about December 21)"
Britanica.com

I love to travel, especially locations that not so many people get to see. In my twenties, I did several Interrail trips where I got to see much of Europe. In addition, I found out about a Nordturist rail ticket which means you could travel anywhere in Scandinavia in one month. I planned to go with a nurse friend, Miranda, and we went on an epic train journey getting a boat from the UK to Esbjerg, Denmark then up to Narvik, Norway the highest point you can get to by train in Europe.

In the summer in Scandinavia, you can stay in many of the schools which are converted into hostels. It's a great way to use these facilities when they are not being used as a school.

It was warm on the trains, but whilst most of Scandinavia had places to stay, we couldn't find anywhere to sleep in Narvik in Arctic Norway and it was freezing, literally. A German guy said we could share his tent but we didn't have the heavy, warm sleeping bag he had, so we didn't last long. We spent most of the night pacing up and down, wearing every item of clothes we owned, waiting for the train in the morning. We didn't mind where it went as long as we were warm!

When we were in arctic Sweden we stopped at a town called Gallivere and went to the local beautiful mission, Stave church. It was Sunday so we went to the church service. We were fascinated to see genuine Lapp people in their traditional clothes that were made with beautiful embroidery and colours. They had not dressed up for the tourists but wore what they had traditionally made and needed to survive the cold. As they were leaving church they adjusted the bobble on their hats so the bobbles faced forward. We learnt that this indicated they were heading home, presumably useful if you are in a blizzard and those you meet need to know if you are heading home.

We later went into the Finnish Arctic and then down the East coast close to the Russian border until we arrived in the Finnish capital of Helsinki. Everywhere we went we tried to eat the local food including fermented fish and reindeer. It was a wonderful adventure.

Reflection:

Being prepared is vital in extreme weather conditions whether it's cold or hot. We should have done our homework before and been better prepared. Nevertheless, it was still an amazing experience I am glad I did not miss.

Resource:

- Sleeping outside in extreme cold: <u>youtu.be/ Vkw8pxr5f9s?feature=shared</u>

Chapter 21

Surviving the Cold War on a Russian Ship

"The Cold War is over but Cold War thinking survives."
Joseph Rotblat

I enjoyed travelling on trains around Europe. Steve, my photographer friend, and I decided to go on an Inter-rail trip. This was where you get a rail ticket where you (anyone under 26 years old) could travel anywhere by rail in Europe for about £100. What adventures we had! We ate cheaply except for each country we went to. We had a typical meal e.g. pizza in Italy. It was a great way to meet some interesting people from other countries. We went through many countries; the Netherlands, Belgium, France, Germany, Bulgaria, Yugoslavia, Romania, Italy, and Greece.

When we were in Paris we ate croissants and smoked *Gittans* and Steve dressed as Quasimodo whilst I took a photo of him with Notre Dame in the background. In Venice we lost each other but remembered that we had said something about meeting on the steps of Venice's Railway station.

When we arrived in Romania it was late at night. We hoped we might get somewhere to sleep but there were no hotels. It was the Ceaușescu Era so not much was available for tourists! We decided to find an office in the railway station so we snuck in one and got into our sleeping bags only to be rudely woken by the kicks of two soldiers holding their guns. Of course, we didn't understand what they were saying but we got the gist.

It was before 6am and we went out into the city. We met a guy called Ionel who spoke English and he kindly took us under his wing. We hadn't realised that they still used food ration coupons. However, he took us to a cafe and persuaded the owner to give us chicken soup. He then showed us around the city.

On our expedition, we had planned to visit Istanbul in Turkey. We loved to see the minarets and the markets and the cross-over between Europe and Asia. One evening we decided to visit a Turkish bath. We both had very rigorous pummelling from a fat masseuse and thoroughly enjoyed relaxing in the steam rooms. As we were leaving we were approached by a guy who made it clear to me that we could go with him and experience more 'Turkish delights'. Although I was pretty naive, I realised that this might not end well so we politely declined. I was glad not to be on my own.

I had previously arranged for us to go on a Russian ship across the black sea to Bulgaria. It was an exciting part of our adventure. As we were shown to our cabin we noticed the restaurant. We were told to meet there at 7pm. As we explored the ship before the appointed time we noticed the restaurant was packed with people. We realised that most people were deliberately avoiding us.

We were disappointed with the way people didn't seem to want to interact with us. We even had to take meals separate from everyone else. We later found out from a Syrian guy that there had been an announcement before we boarded from the captain saying that people were not to talk to us. It was still in the time of the Cold War but still felt very odd. We were just ordinary people and not spies and ironically they were happy to take money for our fare!

When we arrived at 7pm there were just a handful of people! So in the morning we went to the 8am sitting when everyone else went rather than the 9am sitting allocated! Naughty boys.

I recently heard that Ukrainian drones hit a Russian ship in the Black Sea. I wonder if it was the one we went on?

Reflection:

Real travelling requires a certain amount of taking risks but it's worth it. I wouldn't be telling you if I hadn't. As J.K. Tolkien said, "Not everyone who wanders is lost."

Resource:

- Video shows Ukraine's drones hit Russian ship in Black Sea: youtu.be/vZB7nn6rjEQ?feature= shared

Chapter 22

Surviving Buses driving precariously along Mountain roads in Pakistan

"When you share the first cup of tea you're a stranger, the second cup of tea you are a friend and third cup you become family."
Pakistani Proverb

After completing my Child Health Nursing qualification I went to Pakistan and worked alongside a missionary couple, Philip and Florence, in a Christian rural village which was in an area primarily of Hindu tribespeople in a Muslim country. It was a fascinating place to live. The couple I lived with were very much loved by the people.

Philip ran a TB clinic and people walked for many miles to get help from him, and Florence was a midwife. They both spoke Urdu, Sindhi, and Mahalwari languages. Philip and I got around on a motorbike. We were on the edge of the desert. We lived in mud huts and I slept on a rope bed. The first night they gave me an axe as self-defence because occasionally there were 'wild dogs and snakes'. Surprisingly, I still managed to sleep!

Philip taught me how to listen to people's lungs using a stethoscope and we diagnosed many cases of Tuberculosis. Tuberculosis (also known as TB) is an infectious disease caused by bacteria. It usually infects the lungs but can attack almost any part of the body. In this part of Pakistan, it was endemic and fatal. The treatment requires regularly taking a plethora of antibiotics, so it's complicated. We saw children with open TB skin wounds and TB of the spine. I felt useful.

On one occasion we met a group of tribespeople and sat in a circle. As someone who was not used to sitting cross-legged after a while my legs got tired and I stretched them out. This was a definite no-no and Philip scolded me. Later he had to explain to the group that I was from another country, (not India!), and that explained why my language skills and cultural understanding were limited. But they found it hard to understand why I would not understand what was normal to them.

The food was mostly vegetarian curries with the occasional tin of fish or cheese. A couple of times we had a live chicken as a gift from a grateful patient.

During my stay, I received a real telegram from my dad! It said congratulations on passing the law finals. As I hadn't taken law I guessed it meant 'your' rather than law. This was actually my Registered Sick Children's Nursing qualification (RSCN) and I was thrilled to pass it the first time!

One time we went deep into the Sindh desert to an oasis village which was in the middle of nowhere. The women wore beautiful tribal outfits which contrasted with the monochrome of the sand. They looked beautiful, as they dried their clothes by holding them up in the wind. They dried in minutes.

When I completed my assignment I travelled into the Northern areas of Pakistan. I travelled with my nursing/midwife friend, Julie, who was obviously a woman. She carefully covered her head and we pretended that we were married to save the awkwardness of explanation.

However, being a passenger in mountain buses was another experience altogether. I don't know whether it was the fatalistic attitude of the drivers that made them drive the way they did but they didn't seem to be bothered that the mountain drop was so close and the tyres were barely holding onto the side of the mountain. At a couple of places en route, we saw buses and cars that had veered over the edge and were now a heap of broken metal. I would not have done it now.

Reflection:

If you travel and stay in the tourist areas you see the good stuff. If you travel and go off the main routes you see even better stuff. Pakistan is amazing.

Resource:

- Pakistan bus journeys: <u>calamitytravels.-com/pakistan-travel-guides/bus-journey-in-pakistan</u>

Chapter 23

Surviving the spectacular K2 Mountain

"Karakoram Range, the Mountain system, is one of the highest mountain systems in the world; its loftiest peak is K2, at 28,251 ft (8,611 m) is the world's second highest peak."
Britanica.com

The spectacular scenery of the Himalayas, the Karakoram mountain range and the Hindu Kush I can honestly say was the most beautiful scenic area I have ever been in before or since. We flew from Skadu to Gilgit, flying between mountains and past K2 and the mountain ranges. We were not surprised to learn that the pilots were some of the most skilled pilots in the world, carefully moving between the mountains.

We were thrilled when we were invited to the cockpit at the front of the plane and the pilots explained to us the names of the breath-taking mountains we were passing. The cost of the flight wasn't expensive at all and we felt very honoured to have been able to travel this way.

We stayed in small inns with thick blankets to keep warm, all with great views, and we learned that walnuts and apricots were the staple diet for the locals in the winter.

Later we went to Islamabad and I ate a whole leg of lamb to make up for my virtually vegetarian diet in Sindh.

Some of the mosques in Pakistan were breathtaking. The Grand Jamia Mosque, also known as Bahria Town Jamia Masjid Complex in Karachi, is over 2,000,000 square feet and has a capacity of 800,000 people. Entering it when it was nearly empty from the heat and dust of Karachi was spiritually transformative. It was at a different time from the call to prayer and it had a wonderful sense of space and, dare I say it, the presence of God.

However, on our way back south at one point Julie got sick and we decided to go back to the place where I had worked to get some help. The missionaries were upset that I was travelling with a woman and assumed we were in a sexual relationship which we were not. They said that any good that I had achieved whilst I was there, would now be spoiled. I was sad they felt this way but I returned home, having lost a considerable amount of body weight from malnutrition, but with some wonderful experiences under my belt.

Reflection:

I am told that climbing a mountain is an incredible experience. However you manage to get up there to see the tops of mountains, do it. You won't regret it!

Resource:

- Where three mountain ranges meet: youtube.com/watch?v=GZTWKenC6Y4

Chapter 24

Surviving a Knife Attack in London

"Someone once told me that religion is like a knife: You can stab someone with it, or you can slice bread with it."
Vera Farmiga

After my time in Pakistan, I was fortunate to be able to live in the basement flat of a square close to the Oval Cricket Ground. A family lived upstairs and they were happy for me to live in the basement. They were upstairs on weekdays and they were away at their cottage in the countryside on weekends.

I would cycle to Guy's Hospital where I worked as a child health nurse. One day I got knocked off the bike and ended up in a heap. My bike was ruined so after that I had to walk or get the bus.

Shortly after arriving home to the UK, I was walking from my flat to visit the vicar and a guy came up beside me. He nonchalantly reached into his bag and pulled out a large knife covered in a tea towel. He carefully unwrapped it from the tea towel and then pointed the knife at me.

He shouted in an agitated way, "skim your pockets". It took me a while to work out what he meant but I gathered he wanted me to hand over my wallet. I told him I didn't have much and he told me not to "f'ing argue about it" so I handed it over.

I called the police and they took too long to do anything about it. They drove me to the police station and they showed me photofits but I told them I was looking at the knife rather than his face! I did notice he was black and whilst there were hundreds of photos of black guys there were just a few white guys. It felt they were a little biased against the black community.

I would visit my parents in Caterham and they were always supportive of everything I did. On the train back to London was a building with a sign "Take Courage" which I always found encouraging too. I later found out it was an advert for beer!

One time we went to visit some friends and as we left the house a man was lying in his car. We realised that he had experienced a heart attack while he was washing his car. Siobhan and I, as nurses, attempted to resuscitate him but sadly it was too late. We knocked on the doors on the street until we found his wife.

Around that time my dad had a heart attack just after he had been diagnosed with angina. He had chest pain and decided to walk to the GP surgery. Just as he went through the door he collapsed and the receptionist called the GP who was able to resuscitate him. We were glad to hear that he was OK. He needed a coronary artery bypass graft and he survived for many more years.

Recently, my oldest offspring's partner had a heart

attack when they were working on a farm. Again they were able to resuscitate them probably because they were young (around 30 years old). They were working in Scotland at the time and my offspring was in Kent. When they were getting on the train to see him I remembered how hard it was when my dad died before I arrived at the hospital he was in. I offered to go with them or meet them there but they didn't want me to at the time.

Knife crime is on the increase. In the UK in the year ending March 2023, there were around 50,500 offences involving a sharp instrument in England and Wales. Of those, there were 3,775 hospital admissions.

Reflection:

When you walk out the front door you never know what you are going to confront that day. You can't be prepared for everything.

Resource:

- Free first aid training for knife attacks. These are increasingly common and it could be a useful skill to have: <u>first-aid-for-knife-attack.co.uk</u>

Chapter 25

Surviving Jumping out of an Airplane

"I'd rather regret the things I've done than regret the things I haven't done."
Cambodian Proverb

The two experiences of working with the Salvation Army, each of several months in India, got me hooked on working in the Majority South (developing world). I returned to the UK to do further nurse training to become a sick children's nurse at the Evelina unit at Guys Hospital. Again there were even fewer men who worked in the role of a children's nurse. I thought this was sad because I thought, and still think, that boys need good role models of men who care. Why shouldn't boys be given dolls to practise being good dads and uncles?

One time a boy contemptuously asked me if I was gay because his dad had told him "You must be gay", he said, "Because you are a nurse". It reminded me that being gay was somehow wrong and inferior to being heterosexual.

Working in a special care baby unit made me have to think about the ethics of abortion. In the SCBU we were doing everything we could to help premature babies of up to 24 weeks gestation to survive when in the abortion clinic, they were being aborted. Having worked in places where women die because of illegal abortions I knew that the issue was far more complicated than the often polarised view. But rather than being black or white, I choose to be more nuanced on the issue and say that as a public health specialist, we should offer and encourage a wide range of contraception and realistic alternatives to women. There is currently discussion about abortion being performed up to 24 weeks gestation, which seems wrong when babies of 22-23 weeks gestation can survive.

The hospital arranged for a group of us to do a parachute jump following a weekend of training in Kent. It was an amazing experience. Nowadays you are attached to someone else for safety but in those days you were on your own attached to a ripcord but you needed to remember to pull your emergency cord if your main one malfunctioned!

The training was virtually foolproof where you repeatedly jumped from a dummy aeroplane until the routine was stuck in your head. Jump. Count 1000, 2000, 3000, 4000 check parachute. Look up and see if the parachute opened. If it didn't, rapidly pull the emergency cord.

My friend Cathy and I couldn't jump on the appointed day because it was too windy so I had to return to it on a later date. Sitting at the door of the plane you have a choice of whether you are going to jump or not. No one is forcing you. The challenge, for me, wasn't so much the jumping out of the aeroplane but the landing. After you jumped the sounds of the engine disappeared and you were left floating down but then you became aware that at some point your feet were going to hit the floor. The problem was you couldn't really tell where the floor was in relation to where you were so it was just waiting until your feet hit the floor and then rolling onto your side as practised over and over again.

I did it to raise money for the Evelina unit and raised around £3,000. I later heard that the designated person responsible for collecting all the funds had disappeared abroad with a large proportion of the funds, likely including the money I had raised!

After completing my sick children's nurse training, which I fortunately passed on my first attempt, I worked in the paediatric Accident and Emergency department at Guy's Hospital in London. This was catering to an urban poor community. I lived in several locations in South London.

I dated a couple of women but it never went anywhere. One beautiful blond woman friend guessed I was attracted to men and decided she was going to 'convert' me to hetero-sexuality (Being straight). I enjoyed the cuddling but nothing happened in the vital area and I wouldn't have gone through with it if it had but I was curious, even hopeful, that I would be turned on. I knew that she wouldn't have allowed me to go the whole way either but she was sure I could be 'converted'.

In the meantime, I entered a competition for child health nurses where I had to do a case study of a girl who had a congenital malformation on her cheek. I was excited when I was contacted and told that I had won the competition. At the next conference, I was presented with the certificate by a surgeon. He told me that I had clearly impressed the nurse judges, but it was clear to me that he wasn't impressed himself. Although I had been successful, I once again felt a bit of a failure. It seemed as if it was hard to accept positive affirmation but easy to accept negativity. In terms of transactional analysis, I assumed that others were OK and I was not OK.

Reflection:

Doing a parachute jump was a once-in-a-lifetime experience. You either go through with it or you don't... I'm proud to have done it.

Resource:

- Parachute jumping in Headcorn, Kent: goskydive.com/skydive-headcorn

Chapter 26

Surviving the Refugee Camp in a War Zone

"Be the change that you want to see in the World."
Mahatma Gandhi

After my time at Guy's Hospital, I had the opportunity to work for a few months in a refugee camp in Thailand. It was an amazing experience. As I was driven from Bangkok to the border area I was told that the camp itself had been shelled the night before. I suddenly became aware of just how naive I was about the political context and had a crash course in that on the journey from Patty, who was driving me. I was told that the *United Nations* didn't normally allow civilian staff into a war zone but that they had made an exception for this situation so it was very special but we had to be evacuated if anything happened for our safety. I was driven to the camp in the afternoon and received my handover from a nurse who was leaving that evening.

Before I left for the border, Yvone took me to one side

and gave some salient advice. She said that Bangkok was a place where there were many temptations for young men. That they were more vulnerable when they were out of their home environment and to be on my guard against the likely temptations. It is the only time I ever had that kind of orientation and I think it was really important.

I was to be responsible for a large outpatient clinic with a team of 6-8 refugee health workers who had been trained by my predecessors. Once again I was handed a stethoscope and otoscope to listen to chests and look for ear infections. First, the refugee health workers would check patients and then if they needed antibiotics or other medication they were referred to me. So altogether we saw around 200 patients a day and I saw around 30-40. I would refer them to the hospital if I felt they needed to be seen by the doctor. Over the three months I was there I saw thousands of BOM (bilateral otitis media - ear infections in both ears) and diarrhoea that we treated with Oral Rehydration Solution (ORS). I could also use the skills I had acquired in Pakistan listening to chests with a stethoscope to listen for chest infections. Although I did this 'summer of service' for 2 summers I later went back to work in the camps for a further 2 1/2 years.

This was an amazing experience for a Western-trained nurse. We worked under the *United Nations Border Relief Operation* (a subsidiary of UNHCR) and made detailed monthly reports to them. We would carry walkie-talkies with us every day and different situations were called to say how safe we were. The United Nations allowed us to work in this war zone on the condition that we would immediately leave if we were asked to. Situation 1 required us to make sure we had our radios switched on, Situation 2 meant we needed to pack up and leave in an orderly fashion. Situation 3 meant we needed to leave immediately in our 4-wheel drive UN vehicles and Situation 4 meant we needed to 'hit the deck' as missiles were flying in. Most of the time it was Situation 1 or 2. But it was a bit like when I was a nurse working on a ward with people who might have a heart attack. Knowing what to do and how to do it was essential, but it was continually tense.

I loved the community that I worked with in the camps and in the Thai village of Taphraya where the expats lived. It was a caring supportive expat community which really helped with the stresses of working in a refugee setting. We were also encouraged to take a two-week holiday every 6 months which I think was very sensible, indeed essential. We got to see some of the beautiful Thai islands before they became more recently become crammed with tourists e.g. Ko Samui before it had an airport and you could only get to it on a boat from the mainland. Even the trip on the boat was breathtaking.

I was promoted to be the Maternal Child Health (MCH) Coordinator for most of the time I was there. A visiting doctor made it clear that he thought that someone else was more competent to do this role than me even though he was only there for a very short time. Once again my confidence was crushed by a doctor. What is it about some of these doctors that make them feel they can do that? However, I shared a room with Bjarte, a Norwegian doctor who restored my faith in doctors. He was brilliant and kind.

Nevertheless, I was accountable to the *United Nations* and we produced monthly lengthy reports on all that we were achieving (which was not a little). At one point the other leaders were away and I was left in charge of the whole team of around 25 people. It was at a time when we experienced the kidnapping of a UN security officer and a cholera outbreak. It was a challenging time for the whole team but we got through it.

During my time working in the refugee camp, I chose not to think about romantic relationships but to focus on the work. We had a great team of very committed people. Most of the team were women (over 20 at a time) with a varied number of men from 2-4 at any one time.

We were encouraged to read *Henri Nouwen's* book' Compassion: A Reflection on the Christian Life'. I have since read it several times and it has had a profound effect on my life.

The UN Refugee Agency (UNHCR) expects 130 Million people to be forcibly displaced or stateless by the end of 2024, according to the agency's 2024 Global Appeal. That is equivalent to 1% of the world's population.

My house is currently being occupied by a Ukrainian refugee family, a single mum and her two children whilst I am renting a room/sharing a house with my friend, Barbara.

I have recently been involved in creating a flipbook for teachers of refugee children coming to a new country called *'Welcome'*. It has been translated into most European languages where refugees settle.

Reflection:

Working in a refugee camp under the United Nations with a team of Christians was a great learning experience.

Resources:

- Global refugee resettlement needs in 2024: unhcr.org/uk/news/press-releases/unhcr-global-refugee-resettlement-needs-grow-2024
- Where to volunteer with refugees: gooverseas.com/blog/where-volunteer-with-refugees
- '*Welcome*' resource tool for teachers working with refugee children settling into a new country: gmmiles.co.uk/wp-content/uploads/2023/09/WelcomeTalk-A-flipbook-for-Refugee-Children-in-their-host-countries.pdf

Or scan me instead!

Chapter 27

Surviving the Atrocities of Child Soldiers

"In 2021 alone, the United Nations verified close to 23 thousand grave violations against children in the context of conflict. The highest number of violations were 2,515 killings, maiming of 5,555 minors and over 6 thousand children used as child soldiers."

UN 2023

C ambodia is still suffering the consequences of the brutality of the atrocities of Pol Pot's child soldiers 1975-9. If you visit Tuol Sleng Genocide Museum and S21 Interrogation Centre in Phnom Penh you will see photos of victims, but also photos of the child soldiers who tortured the victims in a gruesome way. They are just young teenage children but what they were taught to do was horrific. I once sat in the entranceway to the centre whilst some visitors went inside. There is only a limited number of times you can visit this place. A guy asked me whether it was worth it to visit. It made me sad that he had reduced it to a tourist experience.

When I visited Cambodia in 1990 while I was working in the refugee camps, Cambodia was in a state of depression. With around one-fifth of the population being annihilated in the genocide, nearly everyone had family and friends killed.

People had lost confidence in their country, their communities and themselves. When I was studying public health at the *Institute of Child Health,* Great Ormond Street, one of the professors asked me why I planned to work in Cambodia. She saw it as a place where it would be unlikely that I, indeed anyone, could make a difference due to the country's level of hopelessness. Nevertheless, I felt God was calling me to work there.

In the time leading up to returning to work in Cambodia itself, I was able to visit an incredible project in Thailand with former child soldiers and militarised children from the Thai-Myanmar border. The Government Burmese troops went into the Shann tribal areas killing everyone they found. But some children ran into the jungles and hid. But when they returned to their tribal communities they had been destroyed including their families and friends. Children were then picked up by the rebel tribal soldiers who had been fighting the Government Burmese troops but what could do with them then? They didn't really have a base so children were trained to work alongside them. Some learnt how to cook, others to carry weapons, and some learnt to become snippers. They all learned to survive in the jungle.

The Commander was approached by an American/Shann couple who offered to provide the children with shelter. When I went to the shelter I did research with them to find out what they hoped for. They surprised me by being hopeful in drawings that portrayed their future, and the future of Myanmar. The couple had provided them with a safe place where they felt close to God and each other. The commander would visit and become their surrogate father. They loved him.

It was a huge privilege to meet these children who could once again be children after their horrific time in the jungle. I am sad that in 2024 the situation hasn't changed and the fighting continues.

Reflection:

This was an example where a couple seized the opportunity they had to help vulnerable children. Sometimes we are thrown into a situation where we are given choices to address justice that could make a huge difference.

Resources:

- *Toul Sleng Genocide Museum* and S21 *Interrogation Centre*, Phnom Penh: tuolsleng.gov.kh/en/museum
- *Research Toolkit* I developed with *Militarised Children* on the Thai Burmese Border: gmmiles.co.uk/wp-content/uploads/2013/05/Drawingtogetherhope.pd
- Goins, Stephanie. (2015). *Forgiveness and Reintegration: How the transformative process of forgiveness impacts child soldier reintegration.* Regnum Books International, Oxford: regnumbooks.net/products/forgiveness-and-reintigration-how-the-transformative-process-of-forgiveness-impacts-child-soldier-reintegration
- A summary of human rights reports and insights into global child soldier recruitment: stimson.org/2023/2022-human-rights-reports-insights-into-global-child-soldier-recruitment-use

Glenn Miles PhD

Or scan me instead!

Chapter 28

Surviving Bible College Evangelimould

"Conversion is a complete surrender to Jesus. It's a willingness to do what he wants you to do."
Billy Sunday

T he church I grew up in was very keen for me to go to All Nations Christian College before I did long-term mission/development work, so I went for the interview. I was afraid to be moulded into an 'evangelimould' and hoped I could do just a year's condensed training, but as I walked up the beautiful driveway to the old mansion house I had a feeling I would be there for longer. At the interview, they said that I would be accepted on the condition I would do two years rather than one. It was the right decision and I enjoyed the camaraderie and friends that I made there. As well as a biblical foundation we learned about working cross-culturally and pastoral work. The college supported families so both parents could attend and children could make use of the nursery facilities.

The college invited an 'ex-gay' man, Martin, whom I had met previously and he spoke about how scripture suggested men with same-sex attraction should be celibate. He suggested that some men who 'struggled with same-sex attraction' had successfully entered a heterosexual relationship, while others were content with being celibate. I knew that this more conservative opinion fitted with the stance of the College and I wanted a conventional heterosexual marriage myself. But this was the first time I had become emotionally close to a guy while I was there. I was convinced it was wrong. He may have had similar feelings of attraction to me but we couldn't even talk about it and it felt like only in another universe would it have been permissible for us to be in a gay relationship.

One of the things I loved about All Nations was that I started to really read the Bible and understand just how big God's heart was for justice. The very fact that Jesus came to earth as a vulnerable baby was very impacting and the story of the Exodus had much more meaning having arrived back in the UK, not long after being in a refugee camp.

Whilst I was at ANCC there were a number of women who I was friends with. Again it felt somehow safer to be with them than the guys. But I really wasn't very sensitive that some of the women might be attracted to me in a romantic way. Two of the women on the very same day approached me and asked if we could begin a romantic relationship. I didn't know whether to laugh or cry! They were both lovely people but I wasn't ready for that. Again, it was confusing when I still had feelings for other men.

I was happy to complete my time at All Nations and I made many good friends during that time, some of whom I am still in touch with. I recently attended a reunion and it was very special to see people again after such a long time.

During the course at ANCC, each of us had 6-8 weeks of overseas assignments. I heard about an organisation that worked with the urban poor and was deeply impacted by their writings. I wanted to see what it was like so I asked to join them in Manila and work alongside a guy there, Chris, who was a nurse and also a former student at ANCC.

Much later, I had the opportunity to return to the college to speak about the research we had done on trans-gender in Cambodia. There seemed to be some real concern for this and afterwards, a guy came to talk to me and said that he had been a transgender but was leaving that life-style. He chose to do his overseas assignment with us in Cambodia and we enjoyed him joining the team to do further research with transgender.

Glenn Miles PhD

Reflection:

I am grateful for the time I had at All Nations. It helped me to ask questions rather than be content with simplistic answers. It helped me to confirm my intuitive beliefs that God had a special concern for the poor and vulnerable.

Resource:

- *All Nations Christian College*, Ware, Herts, UK: allnations.ac.uk

Or scan me instead!

- Deconstructing faith - ex evangelicals: premierchristianity.com/features/de-constructing-faith-meet-the-evangelicals-who-are-questioning-everything/267.article

Chapter 29

Surviving Living in a Dangerous Slum in Manila

"If your blanket is too short to cover you completely with your legs straight, bend them so that you fit."
(Learn to adjust to your environment)
Filipino Proverb

I was very impressed by the way the team in Manila (*Servants to Asia's Urban Poor*) lived among the people. It was so different from the refugee camp where with a call on our walkie-talkies we were evacuated at any sign of danger, effectively leaving the refugees to fend for themselves.

The people living in the slums would take any jobs to survive. One of these jobs was to cut the excess rubber from flip-flops for a local factory. It was a laborious job and the whole family was involved, from children to granny. They earned one US dollar for a sack of flip-flops. I helped them for a few hours and I think they had to go over my work before they could be put into sacks.

Living in a slum in Manila was intense. It was clear, Chris really loved his community. One day we were called to a neighbour's house. The mother was weeping because her son had just died. The baby girl had a very high fever so Chris gave her money to take her to the doctor. It was heart-breaking.

Getting back to the slum one evening the tuk-tuk driver refused to go any further into the area because he said it was too dangerous. I then realised the marginalised type of community I was living in but I also knew that people would look out for me.

Chris lived in a small box for a house with a gas stove and pit latrine out the back. He would have a number of boys sleeping on his balcony. One day he told me we would be hosting a boy who was 'on the run' for a crime he, according to Chris, didn't commit. I'm not sure we would have gotten through a child safeguarding audit these days but Chris, rightly or wrongly, was just doing what he thought was the right thing to do and I respected him deeply.

One day I couldn't help but notice a young boy was missing an eye and all he had was his eye socket. He lost his eye to a firework. I decided I wanted to help him and took him into the city. The guy who I was with, Chris, thought it was a hopeless endeavour but I wanted to try anyway. I made inquiries and ended up in a University where there was an Ophthalmology Professor. He was soon to retire and was happy to help without charge. He showed us his wide selection of different brown glass eyes and took measurements. A few weeks later the boy had a new eye! He was so proud! Of course, he couldn't see out of it but he was now not so self-conscious of his appearance.

I was very impressed with the idea of living with people 'incarnationally'. It helped me to develop relationships in a way that would not have been possible if we had lived in the typical expatriate house with barbed wire and guards.

Reflection:

Chris loved his community but it was at a cost. Living with the people was very different from commuting to them as we had done in the refugee camps. I enjoyed the time I was there but could I do it for an indefinite period? We later returned to work with Servants in Cambodia.

Resource:

- Prosthetic Eyes: <u>youreyeinstitute.com/everything-you-need-to-know-about-prosthetic-eyes</u>

Chapter 30

Surviving a Serious Road Traffic Accident in the Philippines

"Life is like a wheel. Sometimes you are up and sometimes you are down."
Filipino Proverb

Chris, the guy I was working with in Manilla, was committed to finding a place to purchase where he could take groups of slum children on a retreat. A group of us hired a jeepney (which is a truck with a jeep front and benches on the inside on either side). Jeepneys were originally made from leftover jeeps after the Second World War. Now they are standard public transport. We took a windy road up into the hills with great views.

But unfortunately, at one point things got out of hand. The jeepney had no suspension and the front wheel fell off the tarmacked part of the road, tilting the truck. To compensate the driver moved the steering wheel in the opposite direction but as the truck hurtled to the other side of the road it made the truck tilt the other way. The driver then had to compensate by steering the opposite way. Each time the tilt was getting further over and finally the whole truck flipped over onto the roof! Now this wasn't a four-wheel drive truck with a bar over the top like a modern Jeep or 4 wheel drive. It had just a flimsy roof but because it was fairly new the roof didn't collapse when it flipped. However, inside the jeepney with no seatbelts, all of us had tumbled over and were left in a heap. At first, it went silent as we all came to terms with what had happened and where we were but then Chris, who had worked in a Swiss army mountain rescue team took control. He waved down several trucks and cars and we got to the nearest local hospital.

Apart from bumps and bruises, most of us were OK except for my dear friend Verena who had fractured her collar bone. They took X-rays and as a nurse, I felt responsible that she was OK. When I finally felt it was all under control I noticed the huge bruise on my side!

When we arrived back to base, one of the leaders seemed more concerned with the state of the new Jeepney than us until we explained to him what had happened and just how lucky we were to have survived, and that most of us only had minor injuries!

For a few days we went to one of the absolutely stunning islands. It was really lovely but the first night we stayed in our beach huts we could hear some very loud lovemaking going on. In the morning two guys emerged from separate huts with their Filipino "girlfriends" who were obviously not girlfriends. They had been competing with each other about who could make the most noise. As I watched them by the pool I could tell that one guy was completely oblivious to the negative side of what he was doing and the other guy felt quite sad, awkward and responsible. This wasn't the last time where I was to be confronted with sex tourists at the time when I needed a break from it.

The overall experience of being in Manila was a positive one. Having worked in a refugee camp where we had to leave at any sign of a problem, it appealed to me to live and work alongside and with people rather than away from them.

Sex Tourism is a major part of the economy of the Philippines, Thailand Cambodia and an increasing number of other countries too (but local exploitation is more common).

Reflection:

Once again angels seem to be protecting us! Something that so easily could have become disastrous was resolved fairly quickly. We didn't take this for granted but were grateful to God for helping us when we needed it.

Resources:

- The history of Jeepneys. See what they look like: youtube.com/watch?v=PopcpDVLmoE
- *Male Sex Tourists*: Sexectations Abroad by Elliot and myself: gmmiles.co.uk/wp-content/uploads/2018/11/Sexpectations-Abroad.pdf

Chapter 31

Surviving Dengue Fever Three Times

"Passion is a sort of fever in the mind, which ever leaves us weaker than it found us."
William Penn

When I returned to Site 2 refugee camp and was quickly promoted to the Maternal Child Health Coordinator responsible for a team of expatriate nurses and hundreds of health care workers who worked in malnutrition clinics, antenatal clinics, as traditional birth attendants, and community health workers.

We also ran a training school for community health workers. In much of the training, we used the vital public health book *'Where There is No Doctor'* an amazing book that has helped train barefoot doctors/community health workers around the world with an understanding that Primary Health Care in villages did not need highly trained doctors but ordinary people who cared about their people and could provide basic health care. Lives could be saved of children with diarrhoea who could be treated with homemade oral rehydration solution, malnutrition could be checked by checking mid-upper arm circumference so children who needed additional nutrition could be prioritised, high-risk pregnant women could be identified and get to somewhere that could help them deliver safely.

But one time when I was listening to a lesson being translated the instructor said how camel milk was important for children. Afterwards, I asked if they had many camels in Cambodia. He said they didn't so we had to discuss how that part of the textbook they were using needed to be adapted to the Cambodian context!

One day I was walking through the camps with one of my Cambodian colleagues, and I noticed a small naked boy. When he saw me he ran away holding his penis and screaming. I asked my Cambodian colleague why he had done that and he said it was probably because some of the mothers told the children that if they misbehaved the 'barang' (foreigner) would chop their penis off! I was a little disconcerted but it was a good way of curbing my ego and any 'white saviour' complex I might have had! I didn't really want to be labelled the foreign monster but I didn't have a choice.

Dengue fever is a mosquito-borne viral illness passed on by mosquitos (which is not uncommon in Southeast Asia). In the refugee camps, we had an extensive campaign to keep water containers covered and a chemical called Abate added. This reduced the incidence considerably. The mosquitos are easy to identify because they are striped and they also bite during the day. Ironically, in the Thai village where we lived, we had a campaign in our refugee camp but there wasn't one outside it, so we were more vulnerable to getting Dengue Fever.

For around 10% of people, dengue is serious and can actually go on to be fatal but for the majority of people it is very uncomfortable, but survivable. I managed to get dengue three times! It causes very high fevers and the body experiences joint pain and pain behind the eyes. It is exhausting. It also has a long recovery period so some people took several months to recover. In our own rooms we had fans but they felt like hair dryers on my hot skin. One time I had the privilege of sleeping in the office which had air conditioning. Overall getting Dengue was an experience I would not recommend.

One time a group of women came to visit us in the refugee camps. They were close friends of one of the nurses on the team. It was nice to see some different folks from home. They had come a bit earlier than expected and we asked them why. They told us that they were on the beach in Thailand and there was a rumour spreading around that there was 'Donkey fever' and that humans could catch it. They noticed a number of donkeys so they decided to leave early! Of course it wasn't donkey fever, it was dengue fever, and they were coming to a part of Thailand in Dengue season. We all laughed hysterically when we realised what had happened!

Reflection:

Some acute illnesses like Dengue create a fever and delirium which leaves you exhausted, but the time it gave me did make me consider the reason we are here on this planet. Sadly, it seems that it is only in recent years, as Dengue has reached the minority South/West, that it is being taken seriously.

Resources:

- Where there is No Doctor. David Werner et. al. *Hesperian Foundation*: <u>warriorpublications.-wordpress.com/2015/03/26/pdf-where-there-is-no-doctor</u>
- Dengue and severe dengue: <u>who.int/news-room/fact-sheets/detail/dengue-and-severe-dengue</u>

Chapter 32

Surviving Gunfire on the Thai Cambodian border

"You must get an education. You must go to school, and you must learn to protect yourself. And you must learn to protect yourself with the pen, and not the gun."
Josephine Baker

Before I had returned to work in the refugee camp I did a Red R course. This included training where we were taught what to do if we were kidnapped. After the formal class where we were sitting in the classroom, some soldiers unexpectedly burst into the classroom and we were suddenly in the scenario we had been learning about! Keep your heads down, don't look the soldiers in the eyes and other salient advice. Even though we knew it was a game it was surprisingly scary. Afterwards we were debriefed on what we had done right and what we had done wrong.

Red R currently runs *Mission Ready: Online security training* for workers on the field. I am sure that it is well worth doing but, perhaps not as alarming as a group of 'soldiers' bursting into the classroom.

Previous to me returning to Site 2 refugee camp one of the women in the team and my friend, Sally, had been kidnapped, but had managed to be released without harm. But it was a reminder that we couldn't take this stuff for granted.

After one day in the camps we were returning to our village in Thailand. We went through one of the checkpoints and heard gunfire very close by. It turned out to be a soldier accidentally firing when the safety catch was undone. But our driver didn't hang around to find that out but got us all to crouch down as much as we could and he raced home as fast as he could!

At one point there was a fire, which was devastating, in a camp made of bamboo huts. The refugees could use the water trucks they normally used for drinking and household use but everything was so dry the fire moved very quickly. Many people lost the few things that they had managed to bring with them when they escaped including precious photographs of families. Heartbreaking.

Another time the refugees were upset by their conditions compared to what they understood the conditions to be in another refugee camp in Hong Kong. They held a 'strike' which effectively made it difficult for us to go into the camp every day. For a couple of weeks, a select group of medics went into the camp under armed guard including Siobhan. Some of the water trucks were unable to bring water into the camps which led to a shortage of water.

This led to a cholera outbreak in which we had to create a special centre where patients could be isolated. Cholera is a devastating illness where the body dehydrates through diarrhoea, so requires rapid rehydration with intravenous infusions. Gloves, masks, wellington boots and scrubs were essential to wear. It was a very intense time.

The village we lived in, Taphraya, was a 'normal' Thai village community but with a few modifications. Of course the main change was the number of expatriates from all over the world. This also meant that there were more places to eat delicious Thai food than usual and an ice cream shop! The village also became a place for rice to be recycled. Rice given to refugees would be exchanged in the market on the edge of the refugee camp, taken to the village and then re-sold back to the UN to give to the refugees!

I remember one time walking through the village and noticing a very handsome young Thai farmer who was walking on the other side of the road. His body was perfectly proportioned, muscular and honed from a life with his back to the sun. We smiled at each other and I sensed that we were both thinking about how different our lives might have been, him seeing me with all the privileges of a white educated man and me seeing him with the body of a god. We smiled and went our way but it was another challenge for me in understanding masculinity.

Thai Buddhist culture meant that dogs would not be euthanized so there were quite a few very scrawny flea-bitten dogs hanging around hoping to be fed, but one very cute dog would chase after the cars as we drove to the camp.

Reflection:

Living in constant emergency-like conditions is incredibly exhausting. For refugees and people impacted by war and disaster, they often do not have the luxury of preparation. They need well-trained humanitarian workers to support them.

Resource:

- *Red R* training for development workers in dangerous areas: https://www.redr.org.uk/Our-Work/Key-Projects/Mission-Ready-Online-Security-Training

Chapter 33

Surviving the Engagement

"Above all, love each other deeply, because love covers over a multitude of sins."
1 Peter 4:8

During this time I became especially close to a woman called Siobhan. What can I say? I grew to love her and she loved me. I had never been really attracted to a woman before but she had become my best friend and I could talk about everything to her. Being in a team and living in a small village in Thailand, commuting to and from the refugee camp was a bit like living in a fishbowl. We had to make secret liaisons just to talk privately.

The first time we borrowed the NGO truck and drove to the checkpoint out of the village where there was a small noodle shop. Not the most glamorous location but it was good to talk. Siobhan was so nervous that just after she sat down she had to go and throw up in the local pit latrine! We quickly headed home and planned our next outing.

One time, when we met on a day off, I sat and talked to her about my attraction to men. She listened and seemed to understand the implications of this for our future. At this point, we both felt that we could 'pray the gay away' and over time my sexual attraction to her would increase and to men decrease.

After only a few months I decided to propose to her. I proposed in a busy malnutrition clinic. It was a symbolic way of saying that if we said yes to each other it was not going to be easy. Our life was going to be complicated. I got an engagement ring and wedding rings made in the refugee camp. The engagement ring had several rubies taken from Cambodian mines in Pailin and given to me as a gift from Siphan, my refugee friend.

Some American friends later told me that it was normally appropriate to spend a month's wages on an engagement ring. Well, I didn't earn anything so it was more than a month's wage! Siobhan didn't mind in the least. It wasn't her style at all to worry about that kind of thing.

I had organised a meal to be provided in the refugee camp. If she said "yes" then it would be an engagement party. If she said "no" then it would be my leaving party! Of course, she said "yes" and everyone was delighted. However the next day I had an awful feeling I had made the wrong decision. I spent the day on my own reflecting on what I had done. It was all very confusing. I worried about the feelings I still had towards men.

I worried a lot about letting her down. I was concerned my self-control would not be enough. At that moment I could have saved her a lot of grief but the many future joys of what our relationship produced would not have been possible. However, we both chose to go through with it and we planned the future.

I called her parents to 'ask permission' which they gave and we called mine too and then went back to complete our assignments. I didn't know until 30 years later that before my mother died and when I came out to my siblings, my mother had wondered why I was marrying a woman when she knew I was gay. This was independently verified by both my sisters.

Reflection:

Should we have got engaged? One friend recently suggested that it was unfair on Siobhan. But we really believed things could change. We were still best friends and our love was real.

Resource:

- Completely mad marriage proposals: thmarch.co.uk/insights/the-10-craziest-proposals-of-all-time

Chapter 34

Surviving the Wedding

*"A successful marriage requires falling in love many times,
always with the same person."*
Mignon McLaughlin

Siobhan wanted us to get married in California,
where she was from, and so much of the preparation
went ahead without us. She allocated different
responsibilities to family and friends. It worked surprisingly
well. She had sent silk to her sisters to arrange for their
dresses to be made. She asked a friend to organise the
flowers etc.

The wedding day was so much fun. Siobhan was quite a
bit shorter than me so I organised for Dr. Bjarte, my best
man, to bring out a step ladder to be brought out from
behind the altar for her to climb up for the first kiss! My
dear friend Dot came from the UK to do a homily for the
wedding. We were reminded of Ephesians 4:12 which says

three cords tied together cannot be broken, meaning that if we had God as the third cord it would help us bond in our marriage.

The reception was held in Siobhan's parent's house and it was great fun! Apart from the usual speeches Siobhan and I performed the coconut dance, a traditional Cambodian dance wearing appropriate traditional silk clothing and clapping together coconuts for the rhythm. I think I was more nervous about getting that right than the actual wedding.

My parents, brother and his family all attended. Mum and Dad went on a visit to San Francisco and walked into an area that was more dangerous than they realised. Kindly the police saw them and took them back to the safer tourist area!

After the wedding breakfast, we went to a hotel in San Francisco where we fumbled around and drank hot chocolate in bed. We later went to Half Moon Bay and stayed in a hotel with real feather beds and drove along the coastline to Los Angeles, stopping at various places on the way. One day we were walking past a volleyball court of gorgeous bare-chested men and we kind of laughed together. I had to remind myself that my desires for men were now a thing of the past. I loved being in California. We stayed in anything cheap and cheerful. We drove all the way down the coast. At one point we ended up in *Disneyland* well before it opened, waiting and chatting for hours in the parking lot!

When we left California we stopped off in Mexico City and went on to visit Dr. Bjarte, my best man who was doing a new assignment in Guatemala. Whilst we were there with him we went to visit a live volcano. The trail that leads to these volcanoes is stunning and the experience of seeing an erupting volcano and lava is unforgettable. Everyone doing the Acatenango and Fuego hike understands that Fuego can erupt at any time and ultimately, even with the presence of guides, you're hiking at your own risk. Surprisingly, in spite of smoke seeping out of the sides and top of the volcano, it didn't erupt when we were there!

We went back through Mexico City to fly back to speak at a missions conference in Kent. We went to the airport and picked up our boarding passes. On the boarding pass was our gate number - eight. We subsequently went to gate eight and were chatting and laughing about everything but after a while I noticed there was no one waiting with us. We suddenly panicked and ran to find someone. A woman stopped us in our tracks. She asked us, "Are you Miles?" in a very French accent; it was the Air France representative, " You see that plane taking off? You are supposed to be on it!"

We had no idea about our rights. The flight board with the gate numbers had not been working. The number was clearly on our ticket but we were being blamed. We were told to come back the following day. We called the conference and they assumed we had arrived and needed picking up from the railway station! We told them we were trapped in Mexico City. They changed when we were due to speak.

We stayed in a 'very basic' guest house and arrived early to be sure we were on time. Of course this time the flight was delayed by around ten hours and we were starting to smell bad. I mean really bad. We finally got on the plane and the French man sitting next to us complained to the air hostess that we smelt bad so she came around with a bottle of perfume and sprayed it all over us. Honestly, I'm not making this up. I am allergic to some perfumes and started to sneeze for the next few hours. The glass of champagne helped a bit.

After this, we travelled back to the UK and I showed

Siobhan many of my favourite places and introduced her to many of my friends. We had a Wedding blessing in the UK so my friends could also enjoy being part of our marriage. Siobhan and I loved being together and genuinely enjoyed each other's company.

Reflection:

I don't believe that getting married to Siobhan was the wrong thing but I also had no idea that our lives were to be far more complicated than we realised at the time.

Resource:

- Trekking to the Volcano in Guatemala: <u>youtu. be/yNk9poOfORk?feature=shared</u>

Chapter 35

Surviving Living in a Pig Farm

"I am fond of pigs. Dogs look up to us. Cats look down on us. Pigs treat us as equals."
Winston Churchill

I n a few short months after the wedding we did an orientation with the organisation we had joined in New Zealand so we could return to work in Cambodia.

Working for the organisation *Servants to Asia's Urban Poor* we had to go on an orientation course in New Zealand. It is such a beautiful country but to keep the cost to a minimum the orientation was held in a pig farm, and it was for 6 weeks. You could smell it from far away and it did detract somewhat from the surrounding beauty.

The accommodation was what might be called as 'basic' but it was a reminder of what we had let ourselves in for. Living simply in the slums.

One thing we enjoyed was getting to know each other.

none

Living and working as a team was going to be important. We learnt a lot about each other.

During this orientation we were interviewed by a psychologist. It was an assessment to check if we were ready to head out to the kind of work we were planning to do. My assessment found that I wasn't ready. The recommendation was that the vicarious trauma of working in a refugee camp had left its mark on me and we needed to take an extended break. If I didn't, the Psychologist told us that something would force us to take a break. This came back to haunt us later. Ironically, although the assessment had been arranged by the leadership they did not take it seriously. They suggested we take a three-week holiday in Thailand on our way to Cambodia instead. We did this and enjoyed our extended honeymoon but it wasn't enough.

Most of the speakers at the orientation were excellent but one guy, Michael, who was a great writer turned out to be a really arrogant person. He lived in a slum for many years but had a really challenging situation where he had to suddenly leave when his slum was bulldozed by greedy landlords destroying the community they had spent years working with. But he somehow gave the impression of being above us- a kind of inverted snobbery. He said if we left, once we had committed ourselves to the slums, then we had failed.

We enjoyed it when we got out of the pig farm and saw one of the most beautiful countries in the world. We got to speak at a range of churches in both North and South Island.

The orientation was partly to build community but also to get used to the idea of living in a slum area. Our later experience however was that most slum houses were well-kept and clean and didn't smell at all. The smell came from the open sewers which often flowed through the communities.

In the orientation we were told about the challenges of living in a slum, but it wasn't what you might expect. Being in a small confined space was hard but when we arrived we had a gas stove, a decent water filter and a pit latrine. Our 'fridge' was a metal box with a large ice block on the side which kept things cool and was replaced by the ice man who delivered most days.

Later in Cambodia I got a pot belly pig for Siobhan for a Valentine's present. I found it when I was doing research in the tribal areas of Mondulkiri. We named him Sir Michael. Siobhan was absolutely thrilled. We made a small home for Sir Michael and the children adored it. One day we found the children reading books whilst lying with their heads on his tummy. We later heard this was unsafe but they were kept safe.

Reflection:

In retrospect it was ridiculous for the organisation to have a psychological assessment if they weren't going to listen to the results. But we were adults and could have made the decision to take a lengthy break ourselves. The caring of carers is a really important part of caring for people working in difficult circumstances.

Resources:

- Providing a home for a pot-bellied pig: msdvetmanual.com/all-other-pets/potbellied-pigs/providing-a-home-for-a-potbellied-pig
- *Caring for Self and Staff - a guide*: gmmiles.co.uk/wp-content/uploads/2017/05/8-Caring-for-Self-and-Staff.-KH-1.pdf

Chapter 36

Surviving Living in the Slums in Phnom Penh

"Negotiate a river by following its bends, enter a country by following its customs."
Cambodian Proverb

After the trip to Manila, I was invited afterwards by the same organisation (*Servants to Asia's Urban Poor*) to lead a team to Cambodia. On an exploratory trip, I had to meet the Royal Government of Cambodia Health Ministry representatives and propose what we could do in a series of concept notes covering supporting the local hospital, working with children impacted by HIV, and working with children with disabilities. Despite some challenges, we were approved by the Ministry of Health to start in 1993!

We entered Cambodia at a volatile time in their history; 1993. The blue-beret United Nations troops were dispatched to different parts of the country to ensure that people could vote and everyone learned about the importance of choosing a new leader. The first time I saw the blue berets was a group from the Australian contingent. I had been working in the refugee camp and had little exposure to this size of men in uniform. As I sat in the coffee shop looking out the window I could see the Cambodians looking up in wonder at these huge muscular guys all over six feet! If these guys were coming to rescue them then everything was going to be safe and fine. It didn't work out like that but I was somehow able to see some hope for the Cambodians which they desperately needed.

The U.N. battalion closest to where we lived was the Indonesian battalion and I spoke to the commander and asked for his help. If things got out of hand could he protect us? He was an honourable man and agreed. He also arranged for his soldiers to paint the clinic we worked in as long as we provided the materials.

The modus operandi of the organisation we chose to work with was to immerse ourselves in the slums so we could better relate to people. We had a small team and after initial language learning and orientation, we all found slum houses to live in. Siobhan and I chose to live in a slum in an area called Chak Angre. We had a small room with a pit latrine outside. We had a gas stove for cooking, an old metal bed, a fan that ran on a car battery, and a couple of cupboards, one for kitchen stuff, the other for clothes. That was it. It was basic but it was our home. We lived in a community of health workers and traditional birth attendants.

Living in a slum was difficult but probably not in the ways that you might think.

We washed our clothes in a large bowl and 'showered' by throwing water on ourselves with a small bowl. We still sweated like everyone else. We had a small fan that ran off a car battery but it wasn't much use, especially in the hot season.

Perhaps the most challenging thing about living in a slum was the lack of privacy. Our neighbours would come and visit us and just sit on a chair in our room watching us.

We had a pit latrine and a decent water filter and were careful about washing our hands, but we still got sick once every 2 or 3 months.

The community was run by a matriarch and everything had to go through her. She was well respected in the community and she had a loud disarming laugh. Often she would come by and see what we were cooking and tell us it was inadequate and then a bowl of food that she had prepared would appear! We felt accepted and learned much about the culture.

The first night we slept on the metal bed it collapsed under us (probably due to the rust). When we told the matriarch she assumed it was because of vigorous love-making in the night and the whole community was told and had a good laugh over it.

We knew that if something serious happened to us we could leave, but we still felt living alongside this poor community enabled us to understand them and communicate better, and therefore be of more use. Of course some people felt that what we were doing was inappropriate but we were getting used to people making wrong assumptions about us.

Reflection:

In retrospect do I think it was worth it to live in a slum? Even though it was not truly incarnational I think it did enable us to build relationships with this vulnerable community. For us it was only a short time but for others much longer. Kristin and Sue Jack brought their children up in Phnom Penh. In one day Sue could be having lunch with the Minister of Health and then go home to her slum community in the evening.

Resource:

- Want to know how to move into a slum?
  servantsasia.org/how-to-move-into-a-slum

Chapter 37

Surviving AK47 Guns at the Airport

"Yes, people pull the trigger - but guns are the instrument of death. Gun control is necessary, and delay means more death and horror."
Eliot Spitzer

At the same time as living in the slums, we were able to support a local hospital that had been recently renovated. At the time we arrived, there was a private midwifery clinic and a private clinic for those that could afford it but we wanted to make it accessible for the poor. We had a medical team of doctors, nurses, a lab technician, and a pharmacist.

We asked that if we taught them to improve their practice and centre, would they help us to make it more accessible for the poor? Initially, they agreed but it took a long time to get anywhere. We later realised they had no intention of helping us.

We conducted a small research project on the local

community but, although it was supposed to be random, we noticed that a certain group (i.e. Vietnamese) were being deliberately avoided. So we made sure that in our future public health endeavours they were not.

On one occasion a boy, around seven years old, brought his mother to get treated at the clinic. She had sepsis and was very unwell. It was by starting the process of helping her that the other staff felt that they also wanted to join in helping. We had a long way to go. We set up a community program for children with disabilities and this worked well. We also ran a malnutrition clinic.

Down the road from us was a small factory. Phnom Penh was hot all of the time and it was an ice-cream factory. There were advertising pictures painted on the walls of delicious-looking ice-creams and lollies. One time we went in to talk to the factory owner. We asked if we could try the ice cream and pointed to the paintings on the wall. He said that they hadn't produced those yet and they had only two types. We laughed with him and congratulated him on his aspirational advertising.

The country was in many ways still very lawless. The police had not been trained well and they were paid so little they had to survive on bribes. The team decided to buy an old jeep left over from the war that was being sold by an expatriate couple who had worked with *Voluntary Services Overseas* (VSO) who were leaving to return to the UK. It was pink. The day we needed to pick it up it was monsoonal rain and the wind-screen wipers didn't work. It was comical to see the team driving through the huge potholes near our house with Siobhan trying to keep the screen clear with her hand going back and forth! Also, it seemed that whenever we went out in the jeep we would be stopped by a policeman and have to pay a fine.

One time when Siobhan and I were getting a flight somewhere, an African man who stood out (as very few around) was asked to open his suitcase as we were checking through our luggage. He calmly did so and inside was a range of AK47s! He handed over a wedge of cash and quickly shut the suitcase and there was nothing else to say. When he realised I had seen he stared at me with a piercing stare and I quickly looked away.

It wasn't quite how I pictured arms trafficking but apparently it worked well if you had enough money and greedy airport staff.

Reflection:

Working in a country that is starting again in many ways from scratch was an extraordinary experience. On one hand it felt impossible. On the other side it felt like anything we did was training people to make a difference and it would make a difference.

Resource:

- Arms trafficking: amnesty.org/en/what-we-do/arms-control

Chapter 38

Surviving the rainy season flooding, drinking sewer water, hand-wound generators, huge rats, flying ants and cockroaches

"People shouldn't be living in certain places [such as] flood plains. But they do, and there are consequences."
Vaclav Smil

O ur retreat house was somewhere away from the challenges of the slums where we could get a shower and sleep on a real bed. But the actual house had a few problems. In the rainy season, it flooded. The owner was actually a mechanic and he had put oil down the drains so when it flooded the drains would create an oil slick on top of the water. The flooding was probably about a foot from the floor and occasionally we would only know after we woke up and found ourselves living on a moat.

The team were resilient and took it all in their stride but one day Sonia said that she still smelled bad *after* she had finished showering. So I checked the well that we pumped our water from and realised that sewage water was leaking through the wall into the well! So we were not only showering in water mixed with sewage but we were drinking it! We had the most amazing silver water filter from Switzerland so none of us got sick but it was pretty sobering to realise what exactly we were doing.

The rats were far too friendly. They were not only huge but it was hard to frighten them off. They would just watch us as we sat on the balcony as if *we* were the intruders in *their* house!

One evening a swarm of flying ants came into the house and Siobhan went around with a spray trying to kill them all. In the morning the helper was upset because flying ants were good at eating and now we had made them inedible! We knew for next time.

The generator had a hand winder to get it going. It required you to attach the handle to the generator, wind it rapidly until it was just about to start and then quickly pull the handle off. One time when it was Siobhan's turn to do it she was accidentally unable to pull off the handle and it flew up into her face. She was lucky not to lose an eye. Fortunately at the time there was a UN German contingent of medics and they were able to help her sew up but she had a lot of swelling for quite a few days.

Siobhan and I had an en suite shower room next to our bedroom. It was very nice to have this and we didn't take it for granted. We didn't have a water heater but you didn't really need it in those temperatures for most of the year. However the downside was that when it rained the cockroaches came up the drain and into the bathroom, and when I say cockroaches, I mean maybe a good hundred every time.

Siobhan absolutely hated it so she sent me into the bathroom with a flip-flop to kill and destroy. I am actually someone who hates to kill any living thing, even insects, but cockroaches and mosquitoes are exceptions. The main challenge when you started was not to get them on your back or inside your clothes. It was satisfying when I had finished. I was the man protecting his wife and I left Siobhan to sweep them up!

Another time a crab crawled up the toilet and would keep coming back after we had flushed it down. People were used to checking their shoes for scorpions but we also had to check our toilet for crabs! It's really true!

Remember this was our retreat house. The place we could escape to from the challenges of living in the slum!

Reflection:

Living in Phnom Penh at this time was an adventure. We had chosen to live there. It is hard for people living there today to understand how much of an adventure it was!

Resources:

- Silver Water Purification: silverinstitute.org/silver-water-purification

Chapter 39

Surviving Pirate Smugglers

"Life's pretty good, and why wouldn't it be? I'm a pirate, after all."
Johnny Depp

Most of the time, we lived in a slum area on the side of the riverbank which was prone to flooding. The traditional birth attendants used the main building to do antenatal and postnatal checkups and deliver babies. We never heard anyone calling out because they were in pain from the delivery.

Sometimes after delivery they would 'roast' the women with a smokey fire under their bed and wrap them up for a few days to recover. The fire wasn't burning hot but it is hard to imagine it would be comfortable. The rest was welcome though.

Siobhan and I slept OK in the slum house we lived in. We got to know our neighbour and over time, he admitted to us that he had worked in the Ministry of Health during the Pol Pot era as an Anti-malaria specialist but was actually now keeping a very low profile. He believed that things could turn bad at any time and I believe anyone who has lived through a genocide of this nature would sympathise with him.

We actually found out that the community we lived in had previously been *Phnom Penh Bible School* and the room we were using was, in fact, one of the student rooms. But it was in a serious state of dilapidation. We had no idea when we first moved into its history. It had been taken over by the Government after the Pol Pot era which converted it into a health centre.

After we had been there some time we realised there was some noisy activity that went on just outside our shutters most nights. When we sneaked a look we saw what looked like an old Russian van. Boats were quietly brought up the side of the riverbank and the Vietnamese 'pirates' emptied the contents into the vans.

We realised with delight that rather than a nefarious business happening, what was being smuggled was actually battery-powered clocks and dried noodles! The boats arrived in the dark and had come all the way from Vietnam. I believe that if they had been caught by the police they would still have been in trouble as no one liked Vietnamese.

After I had cataract surgery, many years later, I got a pirate eye patch and an inflatable parrot to wear on my shoulder. Well if you can't wear one when you are blind in one eye when can you wear it?

In Mumbles, the Welsh village where I now live, they would hang pirates by the lighthouse. The pirate Joseph Avery was hanged near here in 1731. Swansea Bay website says "The Mumbles Lighthouse has guided vessels along the coast, and safely into Swansea Bay for 200 years. It is built on the outer of two islands, known as Mumbles Head. It is often said that the two islands of Mumbles Head resemble a pair of breasts, or 'mamelles' in French".

Reflection:

The slum community we lived in was a lively and caring community. They took us in and looked after us. Our church community close to Mumbles is another community that we feel welcome and have looked after us through thick and thin.

Resource:

- visitswanseabay.com/swansea-bay-at-home/doorstep-detectives/mumbles-lighthouse

Chapter 40

Surviving a Serious Head Injury in a War Zone

> *"Sometimes life hits you in the head with a brick. Don't lose faith."*
> **Steve Jobs**

One night I woke up and Siobhan was experiencing pain in her lower abdomen. At first, we thought it was dysentery or something similar, but Siobhan soon realised it was a miscarriage. We opened the shutters to our small home. The pain continued and the community woke up to see how they could help. Of course I was a man and therefore seen as of no use in such a situation but I didn't want to leave her, so I pulled the bed out and stood behind it whilst the traditional birth attendants did their thing. Unfortunately 'their thing' was to get what looked like a sterilised fire prodder to expel the foetus.

I felt completely out of control and all I could do was pray over her, which didn't seem enough at the time. Unfortunately, to make matters worse, I unhelpfully fell back and hit my head on the wall. This led to me having a seizure where I banged my head against the wall over and over again as I fell to the floor. By the time I reached the floor, I had sustained a serious head injury. My eyes flickered to the right (nystagmus) and I fell in and out of consciousness. A basilar head injury is one of the most serious of head injuries and I had the classic symptoms of clear fluid coming from my ears and later bruising around the eyes.

The attention went immediately away from Siobhan and onto me. The matriarch wanted me to go to the hospital but at that time the hospitals were very poorly run and much too invasive. So Siobhan decided to get me across the other side of town to where Peter, the newly acquired paediatrician in the team, was living. This was at a time when night curfews and the army were monitoring the streets. The matriarch managed to call down an army/police van and persuade them to take us to the other side of town.

Peter wasn't used to dealing with adult-sized people but between him and Siobhan they cared for me. The next day the team came all around to see and pray for me. Daniel stayed up all night to keep an eye on me. Sonia went to the French Embassy and spoke to a neurosurgeon who happened to be there at that very moment. He was wondering what he was doing in what he described as a 'dirty country', but we knew he was meant to see me!

Without any diagnostic tools, he diagnosed that I had fractured the base of my skull. He said if I survived the week I should be taken to Bangkok to receive treatment there but that it would be dangerous to fly before then as it would increase the swelling in my brain. The following day a friend who had worked with us in the refugee camps came by and asked if we had the oxygen necessary to take on the plane. As a nurse who had previously worked to transport patients from Hawaii to the mainland, she well understood what was necessary. We felt that these details were not coincidences, but provisions from God.

So a week later we were headed to Bangkok with a small oxygen tank and arrived at the Seventh Day Adventist hospital. Some friends who we had worked with in the refugee camp visited me and were able to do what the leadership of our organisation did not do. We felt supported and loved by Steve and Marie. The headaches were excruciating and I had become completely deaf in my right ear. My balance was completely 'off' and I experienced tinnitus which sounded like a radio being adjusted. In the meantime, Siobhan needed her own treatment and underwent a D&C to scrape the womb. With little attention on her over the past week or so she had become infected and needed antibiotics.

Three weeks later we were on a Thai Airways flight to London. Our insurance then kicked in and we were taken to a very exclusive hospital in central London. What a contrast! From a slum house to what amounted to 5-star treatment!

By this stage, Siobhan and I were practically joined at the hip. We had lost everything but what we did have was each other. The diagnosis was confirmed and I worked with physios to start regaining my balance using my eyes rather than my ears. After a week or so we decided to go to Burrswood, the healing centre I had previously worked as a nurse assistant. It was lovely to be in a beautiful place where we could re-centre and be prayed for. We were there rehabilitating for 3 weeks. My brother Nick kindly helped with the cost.

The leaders of the organisation we worked with had not

been helpful. They did not come to support us or the team in Cambodia after the accident and did not help us in Bangkok. One of them commented that "the poor had it worse", undoubtedly true but not what Siobhan needed to hear at that time. Then later, just as we were getting back on our feet, I received a letter saying that "when we returned things would need to change". It wasn't entirely clear what was meant by this but it felt like we were somehow being blamed for the accident. When we informed our church of this, we were wisely encouraged by our church to separate ourselves from this group. In fact, it was stronger than that. We were told if we chose to remain with this group then the church would cease to support us!

After our time at *Burrswood* we went to stay with Peter's parents (Dr. Peter being the paediatrician in Cambodia). Although we had dear friends and family who would have put us up (and put up with us), we needed time without them to process what had happened and what we were going to do next. Our hosts were Steven and Peggy.

Steven was a canon in the church. Every year his church had a special service for people who had lost a baby through stillbirth, miscarriage, or abortion. This service allowed our baby to be named and dedicated to God. It was an important time for us to process something which up until then we had very little time to consider. We named our miscarried baby Michael, after my middle name.

We knew that a huge number of people were praying for us as a couple after the head injury. The story became a legend. For years afterwards people (many of whom were strangers) would tell us that they had prayed for us at the time and long afterwards. I believe that it made a significant difference in our healing in spite of the ongoing challenges.

Reflection:

There are things that bring people together that are different from the Hollywood films/Mills & Boon books. Adversity can be tough but can bring you together deeper than anything. We loved each other and I was deeply dependent on Siobhan. Since this happened Servants organisation continues to work in urban areas and a leader actually later approached us to apologise for the way we were treated.

Resources:

- Servants to Asia's Urban Poor: servantsasia.org
- What is a head injury? cedars-sinai.org/health-library/diseases-and-conditions/h/head-injury.html

Chapter 41

Surviving Deafness, Tinnitus, Loss of Balance and Trigeminal Neuralgia

"Kindness is the language which the deaf can hear and the blind can see."
Unknown

I had been diagnosed as completely deaf in my right ear in Cambodia but further tests in London found that my auditory nerve had been cut and I would never be able to hear again in that ear. Most people who are deaf after a head injury recover hearing within 6 months. I never recovered my hearing and hearing aids didn't/don't help. I am impressed with how I have been able to manage with one ear but I am no longer able to hear stereo and I don't know where sound is coming from. I initially also had tinnitus (ringing in the ear). It sounded like a radio was being changed stations all the time. Fortunately it disappeared after a couple of months.

I had to adjust to being deaf in one ear, and my balance was challenged. Going out for a walk in the town was harder than we had considered. Crossing the street required new skills of paying more attention to the cars with my eyes as I could no longer hear so well. When we first went out I held tightly to Siobhan's arm.

I learnt to get most of my balance back with physio and hydrotherapy. Even now after many years, my balance is still challenging in the evening and dark, and when I walk with someone I often walk into them or ask if I can hold their arm. At one point I was crossing the street on my own and walked into a big scary-looking guy. He thought I was deliberately pushing him and was ready for a fight. I had to try quickly to explain that it was due to my head injury. Fortunately, he walked away.

Over the next few weeks, we had to find somewhere to live. My previous landlady in South London heard that we were in need and offered the one-bedroom basement flat I had used as a single man when I worked as a nurse. It was perfect. Siobhan got pregnant quicker than we would have liked, probably because she was healthier and better nourished. Our landlady said that the flat wasn't any bigger but we were still welcome to use it!

At the time I got really low. I went from an exciting pioneering position leading a team in a ministry in what amounted to a war zone to being effectively disabled, living in a rented flat in inner city London with no clear future.

As the pregnancy progressed we anticipated our precious baby and considered names. We chose Zoe (meaning 'new life') if it was a girl and Zachary for a boy. We were grateful to reconnect with the local church community at *St. Stephens church* in Stockwell. I got really quite depressed but was grateful for a loving wife and community.

However, at one point I started getting excruciating

pain in my ear and the pain tracked down my neck. My nerve became swollen and was externally visible down my neck. Initially, it wasn't clear if it was related to my head injury but I ended up in hospital under the neurologist who diagnosed trigeminal neuralgia. They gave me diamorphine (heroin) to try to treat the pain but nothing seemed to help. After a couple of weeks or so, it calmed down but I still have to be careful not to put anything inside my ear.

The vicar, Chris, was a friendly guy and I was impressed by his ability to welcome people of all types from the community. There was a wide ethnicity in the church, people from Council flats to big Georgian houses. One day, Chris mentioned in his sermon about the temptation of accessing pornography 'reaching up to the top shelf" in the newsagent where porn magazines were found. It was the first and one of the few times I heard porn being talked about in churches.

Reflection:

Even though I could still hear in one ear it was harder than I expected to adjust. But it's amazing that I could still manage. God has created two ears for a reason.

Resources:

- Hearing loss following a head injury: jamanetwork.com/journals/ jamaotolaryngology/article-abstract/605567
- *Trigeminal Neuralgia Association UK*: tna.org.uk

Chapter 42

Surviving being an illegal immigrant

"When a foreigner lives with you in your land, don't take advantage of him. Treat the foreigner the same as a native. Love him like one of your own. Remember that you were once foreigners in Egypt. I am GOD, your God".
Leviticus 19:33-34 MSG

I enjoyed going to California. The first time I went was when we were about to get married. I had met Siobhan's parents when they visited her in Thailand but this was the first time I met her friends. After Siobhan picked me up at the airport she took me to meet her friends in their bible study group. They clearly loved her and I wanted to impress but within minutes they handed me some food, pulled their chairs up to where I was sitting and asked me about the first kiss! As a Brit, I felt kind of awkward! I got to know some of them and liked them very much. I was impressed with California's diversity of ethnicities.

We wanted to get a visa for Siobhan to stay in the UK but we were advised that it was better if we applied from outside the country so we decided to visit Siobhan's family in California for a few months. It was lovely to enjoy the sunshine and really connect with some of her lovely friends and family.

We thought about going to do training in Hawaii with YWAM who we had worked with in the refugee camp, so we went to the immigration centre in San Francisco to ask permission for an extension. The immigration officer was intimidating and called me "boy". We asked for a 3-month extension which he turned down so we asked just for an extension to go with our flight home which we had mistakenly got after the visa waiver deadline. He reluctantly said that he would give me an extension but in actual fact he had not. So for a few days I was actually an illegal immigrant! Not something I would recommend.

We did not become aware of this until after 9-11. Although we had returned a couple of times to California after 9-11 whenever I came into the country I was sent to 'secondary' immigration where I was questioned on why I had overstayed my stay. I quickly realised that it was actually better to keep quiet than try to defend myself when I was being questioned.

When I got a new passport I assumed that things would change but they continued. I was told to get a 10-year visa for my passport even though if you have a British passport you are entitled to a 3-month waiver. I did get a 10-year visa and then after it expired I came to the US without one, thinking it would be OK. However, in 'secondary' I was told that I should have got a replacement 10-year visa.

On that particular visit I had an invitation from the US State Department to present research on Capitol Hill so they reluctantly gave me a special humanitarian visa that lasted 2 weeks only and I was told that if I stayed any longer they would come and find me! So I stayed for 10 days and when I got home I got another 10-year visa. It appears that I may be sent to 'secondary' for the rest of my life.

On one visit in which I was returning to the USA from Canada, the immigration official in US secondary kept me waiting so long that I missed my flight and had to get a new one. Meanwhile, Siobhan was waiting at the gate in San Francisco with the children for us to fly together back to Asia. Fortunately her flight was delayed and by some miracle, I managed to race to the gate and join her as she and the family were boarding.

Another time as I was going through immigration I explained to a senior officer that I had overstayed by just a few days around 20 years before. She laughed and said, "Well you won't be doing that again will you?!". "No, ma'am I won't" I replied, and she stamped my passport and let me through without needing to go through secondary.

However, whenever we returned to California we would have the joy of getting Siobhan's friends together. It was a good excuse to have a reunion with her dear friends. I also loved being with Siobhan's family and they, of course, loved seeing our children, and their granddaughters/nieces.

At one point I tried to get a green card to make things easier coming back and forth. We spent a whole day in the immigration centre from around 6am waiting outside until 4pm. As we went up to the counter the officer gave us a date. When we said we couldn't come on that date, she called for the next person, "Next!". We could do nothing but go home.

Reflection:

I have a feeling that if I hadn't been white I would have had a much harder time getting through immigration so I am grateful that although I have had quite a few challenges, I have never yet been sent on a plane back to where I came from.

Resource:

- Unauthorised Populations in the USA: migrationpolicy.org/data/unauthorized-immigrant-population/state/US

Chapter 43

Surviving Siobhan's two complicated pregnancies and near-death experiences of her and our babies

"Pregnancy was probably the best and the hardest thing I'll ever go through."
Mariah Carey

The pregnancy went well up until the delivery date. We decided to go to the cinema in Leicester Square with a friend to watch 'Four Weddings and a Funeral'. During the film Siobhan said she needed to go to the bathroom. She initially thought that her water had broken, but when she checked it was blood. I went to the reception and they called an ambulance and within minutes we were blue-lighted to St. Thomas Hospital.

Although I would love to have been with her, Siobhan suggested to the staff that I should not join them in the emergency caesarean section procedure because the last time I had done something similar, I had fallen over and fractured my skull. So I waited in the waiting room. Siobhan had a very serious condition called placenta abruption and previa, which is where the placenta comes loose and blocks the exit of the baby through the womb causing the baby to not be delivered normally. Siobhan and the baby could easily have died.

Unfortunately we were not impressed with the care given and made an official complaint but as both mother and baby survived, they didn't really take it seriously. It was disappointing but sadly this is one of the downsides of a culture which has consultants who were treated like demigods.

After that, Siobhan took some time to recover. She had been pumped with IV fluids to compensate for the blood that she had lost but swelled up like a balloon. Meanwhile, Zoe was quickly released from the special care baby unit to be with her mummy. Zoe means 'new life' and we felt that it was a new start for us.

Siobhan managed to secure a good job at the *Royal College of Nursing* in London teaching on their first nurse practitioner course. She was very good at this and much loved by the team. We relied on her income as I was unable to work. So maternity leave was limited and she quickly had to return to work after having the baby. So I was left looking after Zoe which I loved, but all the baby equipment in a tiny flat was challenging. We had wanted to go green and use cotton diapers but that became impossible in the space we had. Siobhan expressed milk so I could feed Zoe but that meant she didn't want to take from the breast when she could. As a result, I took Zoe on the tube (underground railway) to where Siobhan worked. It was difficult to get the timing right around lectures but somehow we managed.

One time when I was on the underground 'tube' train with baby Zoe, a man and his son around five or six years old were sitting opposite. The dad spoke to his son and pointed to us, "That's weird isn't it?". It was sad that he was prejudicing his son that looking after babies wasn't a real man's job! I was exasperated but could do nothing.

As I started to feel a bit more able to work I managed to find a local part-time job which was perfect for me. It was setting up a resource centre for parents and professionals working with children with special needs in a children's resource centre in Lambeth. I was grateful to have this creative and interesting job and enjoyed the networking and connecting. Listening to what parents themselves wanted was seen as innovative but, for me, it was basic development that I had learned in my work in the developing world. After working there for a year we had to consider whether to continue to work in the UK or to return to Cambodia or elsewhere.

Siobhan became pregnant a second time and the pregnancy was mostly good until the end again. She had a few false alarms with contractions. In the end, she needed a second caesarean section because Hannah was trying to get out of the place where the previous scar was (scar dehiscence) and once again I was banned from the operating theatre! She lost a lot of blood and once again it was a very serious situation.

We were advised to probably not have more children 'naturally' and that is one of the reasons we decided to seek adoption for our third child.

Reflection:

Siobhan being in such a critical situation was very disturbing. Once again everything was out of our control, so all I could do was to pray. We were also once again grateful for the prayers of friends and family.

Resources:

- Placental Abruption and Privea: nhs.uk/pregnancy/labour-and-birth/what-happens/placenta-complications
- Caesarean scar dehiscence: ncbi.nlm.nih.gov/pmc/articles/PMC6293899.

Chapter 44

Surviving Failure

"Failures, repeated failures, are finger posts on the road to achievement. One fails forward toward success."
C. S. Lewis

After three years I completed my nurse training in London. I had lost my confidence in taking examinations doing my A levels and didn't do very well with the course mock examinations but I was deeply disappointed when I failed one part of the final examination. It was hard for my friends to celebrate when I hadn't passed but their support helped me through it. It wasn't easy to fail in a context where nearly everyone passed.

I took the exam several months later and passed but I grieved my failure and wondered whether I was really clever enough to be a nurse.

After I finally graduated from general nurse training I became a registered general nurse. I was obliged to work in the hospital in the private wing, the complete opposite of my experience in India. I had the privilege of caring for an Arabian princess and also the famous actor Laurence Olivier.

When I was looking after the princess, her sister (also a princess of course) lost her watch by leaving it in the staff bathroom. It was a gold diamond studded watch and I don't think it was ever recovered. I informed the chief nursing officer who told me to inform the police. A bobby (junior policeman) turned up rather amused. When the crown prince heard what I had done he was furious, "If we've lost it we've lost it. We just need to be more careful in the future" was his response. He didn't want negative publicity and money was not an issue even after losing a £14,000 unique diamond-encrusted watch.

I still had a few close friends who were women but not many close male friends. In one of the shared houses I lived in was a well-built Christian guy who was very popular with girls. He worked out at the gym and was friendly and secure in his heterosexual identity. I thought he was gorgeous but had to keep my feelings to myself. Once he asked me if I was gay but I refused to admit it. Nevertheless, I appreciated that he respected me enough to talk to me.

Much later when I was in my late fifties, I tried to get my child health nursing qualification restored as it lapsed in Cambodia so I did the retraining at a local hospital. It required working in a unit where children in medical crises were initially seen. I loved the face-to-face caring for children and their parents, but it was 30 years (1987-2016) since I had qualified and I had not worked in a hospital since.

Of course, technical things had changed massively but harder to understand was the way everything was done with the attitude that the hospital, or you, could be sued if you did something wrong. They were simply not willing to take on the risk of having me work so I didn't get through the process. It was sobering to get a Failure letter through the post from the same University that had given me a PhD. Once again I was reminded that I could not/should not see my value in labels, but rather in the fact that I am made in the image of God and loved by him.

When I had my head injury I was unable to drive. I had already tried, unsuccessfully, to learn to drive on several occasions. After the head injury, my spatial awareness was impacted. I was able to learn to drive again later but failed again. I can't even guess how much money I have wasted on driving lessons and I still can't drive.

Reflection:

Despite the challenges, nursing is still a fantastic way to begin a career. It gave me confidence in dealing with people from birth to death, managing a complicated ward and supporting people in crisis.

Resources:

- Starting a career in nursing: <u>healthcareer-s.nhs.uk/we-are-the-nhs/nursing-career</u>
- Coping with failure: <u>rehab-recovery.co.uk/articles/10-healthy-ways-to-cope-with-failure</u>

Chapter 45

Surviving Success

"Smart people learn from everything and everybody. Average people learn from their experiences, stupid people already have the answers."
Cambodian Proverb

In 1995 I was awarded the Robert Tiffany International Nurse of the Year award from the *Royal College of Nursing* and the *Nursing Standard*. It was a huge privilege for the work I had done to be recognised. I also got two scholarships that provided funding to do a Master's degree from the *Smith & Nephew Foundation*, and the *Hospital Savings Association*.

I began a Master's in Maternal Child Health at the *Institute of Child Health* (part of *Great Ormond Street Hospital* and the *University of London*). I was the only English man on the course but it was a great opportunity to learn amongst a wide range of people with nationalities from around the world, many of whom received scholarships from the British Government. The course was well established and I learnt research skills which proved to be very useful and also the importance of advocacy and being political. Of course, I already had the practical experience of doing the topic from my real-life experiences in the refugee camp, so it all made sense.

Part of the course was conducting a research project in Newcastle. I was partnered with a Muslim Palestinian guy, Suliman, and our research was looking at the nutrition of Newcastle school children. School dinners were not so nutritious then and dispensers in the corridors were selling sugary soft drinks and sweets. We were able to make recommendations to the schools and got our research published in the *Nursing Times*.

When I graduated I was surprised to receive a distinction grade which I had not expected at all. It showed me how important the environment is to your self-esteem and success. In school, I had scraped through only one A-level exam, and then again in Nursing school, I failed the first time. However, studying topics I knew about and was passionate about, such as public health, made all the difference and I excelled above and beyond what I thought was possible for me.

In 1986 I also won the *Robert Tiffany International Nurse of the Year* award for the work I had done in Cambodia and how I had used my experience in developing the resource centre in Lambeth. It was awarded by the *Royal College of Nursing* and the *Nursing Standard*.

During this time, we were able to get a mortgage for a small flat in London and became part of the lively and multicultural St. Stephens Church community in Stockwell.

After this, I was offered a job with the NGO *Tearfund*,

a Christian relief and development agency. I was initially given the job as a desk officer which mainly involved processing proposals for South Asia. I was keen to show my abilities. I enjoyed working for an organisation that saw the importance of advocacy and its role in educating the church on important issues. For example, they were well ahead of the curve regarding HIV/AIDS and Climate Change. I was getting back on my feet.

After this I asked Siobhan what she would like to do, having focused a lot on my needs over the past few years. She said she would also like to attend *All Nations Christian College* where I had previously gone. So we lived outside the College in a small flat in Ware, where I would work as a consultant mainly for *Tearfund* and she would study.

Sometimes, I would travel abroad which would leave Siobhan, as what she described, a single mother (!) but I refused to stay away for longer than two weeks every two months. She would say to her friends jokingly that I went to exotic countries whilst all she went to was *Tescos* supermarket! But I knew she was as gifted as me, if not more so.

Reflection:

After all the trauma we had experienced it was good to experience some positive recognition of what we had done.

Resources:

- University College London Institute of Child Health MSc. Community Child Health training: prospects.ac.uk/universities/ucl-university-college-london-3871/ucl-gos-institute-of-child-health-30208/courses/paediatrics-and-child-health-community-child-health-msc-145029

Or scan me instead!

- Tearfund UK: tearfund.org

Chapter 46

Surviving Sri Lanka's Beaches

"On this big ball of people, I'm just one grain of sand on this beach."

Aurora

I t seems an odd thing to talk about surviving some of the most beautiful beaches in the world but the reality for many Sri Lankan boys was that they were desperately doing anything they could to survive, which included selling their bodies.

One of the countries I visited/consulted with Tearfund was Sri Lanka, which was (and still is) known for the sexual exploitation of boys and young men. Tearfund was ahead of its time in supporting the organisation ESCAPE which was impressively doing prevention, advocacy, and aftercare. They wanted to address the fact that boys were being sexually exploited on the beaches and that the police were arresting the boys and leaving the perpetrators to sunbathe on the beach!

As well as recruiting the local banks to fund a campaign to raise awareness about the issue they had written an article for the local Sunday papers and, as a result, were invited by the Prime Minister to make recommendations on what to do about these boys. A fantastic opportunity that resulted in the development of the *National Child Protection Authority* (*NCPA*).

They also had a small centre called *Kadella* ("nest") to provide safe and supportive short-term residential care. As well as evaluating the program I was able to do research with children in the schools in high-risk areas and got my first research paper published in the peer-reviewed journal, *Child Abuse and Neglect*. The title was "Children don't do sex with adults for pleasure" which was a quote from a schoolboy which said so much.

Another thing I was impressed with was that when the staff went to churches to tell them about the sexual exploitation of boys on the beaches, they started to hear more and more stories from church members about leaders in the church who were sexually abusing. I felt at that stage they could have stuck with the 'easier' topic of sexual exploitation on the beaches but they chose to enter the very challenging issue of child protection in churches. For a while, ESCAPE's project was my idea of an ideal one that involved prevention, advocacy, aftercare, and rehabilitation.

I later visited Sri Lanka after the tsunami which affected one whole side of the island. There were boats up off the side of the beaches and whole villages destroyed. It caused a deep depression among the communities there. I heard a wonderful story of an NGO (charity) who had gone to one of the villages to talk to the adults to see how they could help, but the adults who were too depressed sent them away. As they were getting into their car they noticed a group of children sitting on a wall. They decided to talk to them instead. This resulted in an unexpectedly useful meeting. The children had very clear and sensible ideas about what needed to happen, in particular they suggested that the buses should be reinstated as soon as possible as this enabled the adults to get into town to shop, trade, find alternative work, get to the health care centres etc. Such a great idea and it happened because people trusted that children would understand the needs of their own community.

I loved being a dad. When I returned from a trip the children learned to sit on the couch and shut their eyes with their hands out waiting for the small gift they knew they were going to get. On one occasion Zoe asked me, "Are they better now Daddy?".

"Who darling?" I enquired.

"The children you went to help". It seemed like it was acceptable for me to go away as long as I was helping other children! I truly wished 'helping' was that simple!

During this time I helped to write the *'Tearfund Children at Risk Guidelines'* for program managers of partners of *Tearfund* which were based on case studies of existing partners and a Biblical approach to child care. I also did project evaluations, most of them in Asia.

The plan was after Siobhan had completed college we would go to work in Cambodia with a partner organisation of *Tearfund* in an advocacy role. Sadly the role changed and the offer was withdrawn. So, although we were all ready to go with packed boxes, we had to re-think what we were going to do.

I recently returned to Sri Lanka to work with Bandara who had a deep concern for marginalised children in the rural tea plantations which had been originally planted in colonial times, but are still there after 200 years. We did research for him to encourage the government to provide more resources for these children. We also started a GoFundMe campaign to build an additional classroom, a play area, and to fix the toilets.

Reflection:

Tourists are not the main cause of sexual exploitation but they cannot be ignored. Sex tourists often focus on countries where if caught they could bribe their way out. Countries need to be sure that tourists understand that if they "abuse a child in this country" they will "go to jail in yours" (this was a poster campaign in Cambodia).

Resources:

- *Tearfund Child Development Study Pack* - see the Case Study on LEADS in Sri Lanka: gmmiles.co.uk/wp-content/uploads/2013/05/ Childdevstudypk.pdf

Or scan me instead!

- *Tea Plantation School* extension project. GoFundMe fundraising project: gofund.me/ 690d11b4

Glenn Miles PhD

Or scan me instead!

Chapter 47

Surviving Posh Tunbridge Wells Spa Town

"There's a difference between being posh and being rich."
Kate Reardon

T unbridge Wells is a beautiful yet expensive town and not somewhere we ever imagined living. It seemed far too posh and we didn't have much money! When we explored where the children could go to school it quickly became apparent that there was the *right* kind of kindergarten so that children could go to the *right* school where they could get into the *right* kind of university. Very stressful for young parents.

After leaving ANCC we had to find somewhere to live. We found out about a retired missionary who lent us her home in Tunbridge Wells for a few months while she travelled. It took longer than the time she was away so from there we moved to a terraced two-up-two-down house where we had a 'peppercorn' rent. We paid just one pound a month in rent which was extremely generous of them. With very little money it was enormously helpful.

Our landlord was a retired dentist who had bad arthritis in his hands. His wife told us that he insisted on making tea for her and bringing it to her in bed. But the only way he could do this was by putting the cup in a bucket and carrying it in his teeth up the stairs. What a guy!

In the meantime, I found a job at the *Job Centre* for Siobhan and she worked part-time as a night nurse in the *Overseas Missionary Fellowship* (OMF) nursing home. It was an amazing place to care for ancient missionaries who were some of the original *China Inland Mission*aries. They would pray, and fast, and I do not doubt that the world was changed through their prayers, but Siobhan had to scold one diabetic lady for fasting while she was praying!

I did some work with *Viva Network* developing the Celebrating Children course including their workbooks. Really great organisation connecting organisations working with children around the world.

In the meantime, I started my PhD in Childhood studies at *Swansea University*. I had to attend lectures 2 days a week for 2 terms and stayed overnight from Sunday to Tuesday. I stayed in a bed and breakfast and the owner got to know me. One day he teased me that my wife had called and he had told her that I was out entertaining a blond woman. Siobhan didn't believe him. Well, he thought it was funny.

My supervisor Nigel said that if I returned to Cambodia to do my research he would be happy for me to keep in touch with him via Skype/Zoom and e-mail, and try to meet him in person every year. If he hadn't said that it would not have been possible.

At a *Viva Network* conference, I met the International

Director of *Tearfund* and she once again opened the doors to the possibility of working in Cambodia. This time as the Children at Risk Facilitator. This meant identifying projects that fit with *Tearfund*'s modus operandi, and then capacity building including developing networks. Also, I could continue my PhD fieldwork!

Reflection:

Sometimes when you think it's all falling apart you find things (with God's help) slot together and work out better than it would have been if plan A had 'worked out'!

Resources:

- Visit Tunbridge Wells: visittunbridgewells.com
- *Viva - Together for Children*: viva.org

Or scan me instead!

Chapter 48

Surviving our Children being Kidnapped

"See that you do not despise one of these little ones. For I tell you that their angels in heaven always see the face of my Father in heaven."
Matthew 18:10

S ome people thought we were crazy to even think about returning to Cambodia especially now we had our two children, Zoe and Hannah. We had also gone through the process for an international adoption. We loved *Tearfund*.

Being the Children at Risk Facilitator was an exciting role and one I enjoyed very much. Returning to Cambodia we were welcomed back by friends and colleagues. Within a short time of arriving, we were pretty well established. Siobhan secured a role working with the Catholic NGO *Maryknoll* in their HIV program. Her nurse practitioner skills were invaluable.

This was a time when many parents were dying of HIV,

leaving many children orphaned. One of the organisations we supported was the *HALO* project, an excellent foster care program that is still modelled today. This project evolved into the *Alongsiders* program which is now a global phenomenon. Other programs included one by an extraordinary man with disabilities who managed an NGO for children with disabilities. His example was a shining role model for children and parents who had thought that all children with disabilities were cursed.

Tearfund allowed me to use part of my time to do the fieldwork for my Ph. D. research on *'Cambodian Children's Understanding and Experiences of Violence Involving Children'*. We conducted a series of focus groups with children using pictures and asked them to role-play what happened. I then trained our small team and we visited every province in Cambodia doing surveys with boys and girls from schools in every province in Cambodia.

In the end, we had a total of 1,314 child participants. Most national surveys are done in a few 'representative' provinces but doing it in every single province was much more interesting, and more representative. At one point my supervisor, Nigel, from *Swansea University* came out to Cambodia and we travelled on a small 4-seater plane to Ratanakiri to do research with children in the tribal areas. So cool. Nigel loved it and I earned brownie points for arranging that.

We also produced a series of workbooks in Cambodian with locally produced songs on a DVD using puppets to teach children about keeping safe. Everything we did was in collaboration with other organisations to get the best use of the money we had available and to create ownership. Sir Cliff Richard came to visit as an ambassador for *Tearfund* and sang 'Living Doll' which was thought to be very appropriate. It was fun to meet him. He actually came to dinner at our house. How many people can say Cliff came to their house for dinner?

During this time in Cambodia, Siobhan loved working as a nurse practitioner for *Maryknoll,* a Catholic agency. Her focus was on caring for people with HIV and this was when many people were dying before medication was available. Later she had to give this up to do all the necessary running around for us to do the adoption process for our precious Sarah.

Walking on the streets was an adventure in itself. Very few expatriates lived in Cambodia with their children at that time, so people were completely enamoured by the children, Zoe being a redhead and Hannah with her little fat cheeks. Mostly we just smiled but every now and then someone would grab hold of one of the children and 'kidnap' them, taking them to the back of the shop or running away to show them off to someone, usually a relative. The first time was particularly alarming but when we realised what was going on we were a little more careful. Apart from anything else we didn't want the children being afraid of the people we had come to serve by being taken away from us.

Talking of which one time when we were at a traditional Cambodian wedding, Hannah was pinched hard on her very chubby cheeks by someone who wanted to see what it looked like for a white girl to cry. Siobhan went over to the woman and told her that we didn't appreciate her being pinched like that. When mummy came back to the table, Hannah said "Not that lady mummy, that one" and pointed to someone else. We hurriedly made our exit.

The recent movie *'The Sound of Freedom'* gives the impression that their version of trafficking involving the actual kidnapping of children who are taken overseas is what usually happens, but the reality is very different. Trafficking is where a person/child is sold as a commodity.

According to the UN "Trafficking in persons" means the recruitment, transportation, transfer, harbouring or receipt of persons, by means of the threat or use of force or other forms of coercion, of abduction, of fraud, of deception, of the abuse of power or of a position of vulnerability or of the giving or receiving of payments or benefits to achieve the consent of a person having control over another person, for the purpose of exploitation. Exploitation shall include, at a minimum, the exploitation of the prostitution of others or other forms of sexual exploitation, forced labour or services, slavery or practices similar to slavery, servitude or the removal of organs".

Reflection:

Our children were not kidnapped, thank God, but it did make us think about just how many children are trafficked every year in Cambodia and throughout the world. Child Trafficking is now a major part of what I am researching, primarily listening to the voices of survivors.

Resource:

- *Sound of Freedom* Movie:
  imdb.com/title/tt7599146

Chapter 49

Surviving the Cambodian 'Wild West'

*"Every time I see something about the Wild West, I'm
reminded that our version of history may not be what really
happened."*
James McBride

On the Thai-Cambodian border, on the other side
of the border of the place where we had previously worked in the refugee camps, was a place
called Poipet. It was a very difficult place to get to until they
fixed the roads. The potholes were enormous and could take
11 hours to arrive there from Phnom Penh. When you
arrived it was a dusty dry road that crossed the border into
Thailand but it had a very real sense of being a dangerous
place. The extreme poverty was palpable.

On one side of the border in Thailand was a busy
marketplace where Cambodians could cross to sell products
they had, but mainly to buy products. They were permitted
to go for a few hours, or for a few months if they had a

special licence. Many Cambodian children learned how to illegally cross the border to sell cigarettes and other products. Other children would push carts that were often large enough that they should have been pulled by horses.

On the Cambodian side of the border a group of buildings emerged which were places to gamble in stark contrast to the surrounding poverty. There were large buildings with air conditioning and large screen TVs showing horse racing at New Market, in fact everything you might expect in an international casino centre for gambling; slot machines, card games and roulette. Many of the punters/sex buyers, we were told, were wealthy women from Bangkok. Some were men. They were unable to gamble in Thailand so this was a way around the law.

We worked with the organisations that were working on the border and created a map of where children were being exploited. It was disturbing just how many ways children could be exploited in what amounted to around one square mile. One of the most disturbing groups of vulnerable children was the 'umbrella children'. These were children who held umbrellas for punters/sex buyers who came to gamble to protect them from the bright sun. They would take them to their hotels. However, we found out that many also provided sexual services to the gamblers too.

Poipet was similar to the Wild West towns you see in movies. Not the cowboys but the muddy streets. When it rained, it poured and the potholes were huge. One time I was on the back of a motorbike getting around the town and a large truck drove past. The mud from the wheels splashed me so I was completely covered from head to foot in mud but the motto driver seemed to have got away with hardly any mud at all. People who saw it tried very hard, but unsuccessfully, not to laugh. After the shock, I laughed too and quickly went back to the guest house for a shower.

The gambling area expanded and former refugees who had repatriated back into Cambodia, who were living in the area closest to the official border crossing, were evicted from their homes with nowhere to go. So many went along the border areas to the least desirable areas - places which still had landmines years after the Khmer Rouge was disbanded.

There were varying levels of tension between Cambodia and Thailand. At one point the border was closed. A deeply troubling situation occurred when a disabled boy was left at the border. Disabled children were trafficked across the border to Bangkok where they were used to beg for money in strategic locations around the city. As the border was closed he was no longer of any use, so was abandoned. Siobhan and I seriously considered whether we might adopt him but an organisation in Phnom Penh that had taken in a number of children with learning difficulties were equipped and willing to take him.

Poipet has become increasingly used by backpacker tourists who want a cheap way to access Cambodia from Thailand. They don't mind the time it takes and don't want the cost of a flight. The time it takes to get to Phnom Penh has reduced from 12-13 hours through pot-holes as large as a car to 4-5 hours on a smooth highway.

Reflection:

Some places have a palpable sense of a traumatised community. Poipet seemed to ooze the feeling of people being exploited in so many ways through poverty, exploitation and slavery.

Resources:

- Crossing the border at Poipet: <u>planetgravy.-com/cambodian-borders-poipet-scoop</u>
- US State department Trafficking in Persons report of Cambodia: <u>state.gov/reports/2023-trafficking-in-persons-report/cambodia</u>

Chapter 50

Surviving Landmines

"Incapable of distinguishing between the footfall of a soldier and that of a child, antipersonnel mines cannot be aimed. They indiscriminately kill or injure civilians, aid workers, peacekeepers, and soldiers alike. They pose a threat to the safety of civilians during conflicts and long afterwards."

Int'l Campaign to Eradicate Landmines

Landmines are one of the scourges of Cambodia. There are over 40,000 victims who have lost their limbs, one of the highest per population in the world. About four million unexploded landmines and munitions were removed between 1992 and 2018, but demining efforts are still ongoing. Despite years of concerted clean-up efforts, from organisations like the Cambodia Mine Action Centre there still is more than 386 mi^2 (1,000 km^2) of Cambodia that is still unsafe.

One charity, called APOPO, trains giant African rats to use their incredibly powerful sense of smell to detect landmines in the countryside. They are so clever at this that the rats can dart through a field quickly, covering far more ground in a day than can a human with a metal detector.

For the refugees, many had walked through minefields in order to escape Cambodia. We were taught about unexploded ordinances (UXOs); mostly how to avoid them. This meant not wandering off into the bush to pee but using the back tyre. Sometimes we were required to be in a convoy where 3 cars would follow each other as a means of security.

One time in Site 2 we went to a section of the camp where survivors of landmines were put together. It was a sad sight. The cultural perspective that bad things happen to bad people doesn't help. I felt helpless and I asked how we could pray for them. One guy said please pray for my heart. I was deeply touched that he had chosen that over praying for something else.

We did mapping and research with children in the area to help organisations to understand the context better. I went with Chom No who worked in Poipet with the Cambodian *Hope Organisation* and he pointed to a tree where a pile of mines had been extracted from the ground so that people could build new homes. It was terribly unsafe but when people are desperate they have very few choices. NGOs who cleared mines focused on Government land. The owners of these areas of private land were supposed to pay for de-mining, but of course they did not.

Chom No arranged training for teachers throughout the whole province, teaching them how to use the *Good Touch Bad Touch* flipchart to help protect children against exploitation.

We later worked with border guards doing training in child rights so they understood that their responsibility was to protect children, and not punish them.

Reflection:

It is hard to get your head around people creating mines so that people are maimed rather than killed. Some landmines are actually designed to look like toys so that children pick them up. **Lord have mercy.**

Resources:

- *Cambodian Mine Action Centre*: cmac.gov.kh
- The Landmine Ban Treaty: icbl.org/en-gb/the-treaty.aspx
- *Good Touch Bad Touch* flip book: good-touch-bad-touch-asia.org

Chapter 51

Surviving the Orphanage Scam

"What if someone causes one of these little ones who believe in me to sin? If they do, it would be better for them to have a large millstone hung around their neck and be drowned at the bottom of the sea."
Matthew 18:10

S adly, within a few months of arriving we were enmeshed in a terrible situation involving an orphanage. We were invited to visit the orphanage by an expatriate couple and within a short time we realised there was a lot more going on than was obvious. One local woman was responsible for around 12 children (24/7) with no help. We wrote to the 'donor', Benjamin, and he accused us of trying to make money from adoptions. We wrote to donors on the website and they thought that Ben was the nicest man and so kind to the children.

Meanwhile, he had barely given enough money to pay

for food for the children and not enough for medicine when they were sick. If he had increased the amount he gave and improved the situation for children we would probably have let it go but as we looked further, problems were exposed. We heard a rumour that some of the children had been brought from a hospital by poor women, and that other children had died and had been buried in the back of the orphanage. We did not have proof that either of these was true.

But then one time I was having lunch with Joke (pronounced Yoka), a friend from the Netherlands, and she heard me talking about Ben on the phone. She said that she had heard about him but had never met him, but her church supported him. Ben had sent the church pictures of children that they were supporting from the orphanage. The problem was none of the children they were sent pictures of were actually in the orphanage. We did some investigating to find this out and it turned out that the children were in the community surrounding the orphanage, but not in it. One day someone (Ben) had come to the village, and asked if they could take the children's photos in exchange for 10 kilos of rice per month. They never saw him again.

We had exposed a big scam and in the middle was a small group of children who were being badly neglected. Lots of money was being taken from various churches around the world but most of it was going into the pockets of Ben, the head of the organisation. We longed to help and took our evidence to the *UN Human Rights Office*. They made recommendations about what needed to change but it mostly ended up being ignored.

We had sought help from a senior church official but he reacted badly, listed his face, and took it personally. It was a lesson in the importance of loss of face in this culture. The church official also was being backed up by expatriates who should have known better. I was 'interviewed' by a panel of people who were apparently neutral except that they weren't neutral at all. I was accused of 'trying to destroy the Cambodian church'. The church leader appeared to be more upset about his reputation than these precious children's lives. I remember being in tears over it, not understanding how someone like Ben could be so corrupt and could still 'win'. It was an important lesson for me that God would not always intervene in ways that we would like.

Representatives from *Tearfund* followed up after this happened and were concerned about me and my family. They kindly sent us on holiday for a week in Vietnam to take a break from this traumatic event. My parents were shocked that going to Vietnam could actually be a place to take a holiday, but we had a great time.

Rethink Orphanages suggests:

- Globally, over 80% of children in orphanages have a living parent.
- Up to 8 million children are thought to be living in orphanages.
- Children who grow up in orphanages are at much higher risk of becoming victims of violence, trafficking and exploitation.
- Care leavers face a higher risk of homelessness, mental health challenges and suicide.
- In many countries, income from donations and volunteering is driving the rise in orphanages.
- Orphanages can be up to 10 times more expensive than caring for a child in a family.
- There is a global effort to end the use of

orphanages. Every country in the world must be committed to family-based care.

Recently there has been serious concern about the number of orphanages with volunteers, 'orphanage tourism', which can be used both for the exploitation of children and tourists.

Reflection:

Tens of thousands of churches around the world still support orphanages because it seems like a good thing when realistically many children in orphanages are not genuine orphans, but are being used to generate money. Churches need to do careful assessments before they provide help, and do careful screening of volunteers before visiting them.

Resources:

- Rethinking about orphanages; how they can be exploitative: <u>rethinkorphanages.org/school-university-groups/information-about-orphanages-facts-about-orphans-statistics</u>
- Challenging orphanage tourism: <u>thinkchildsafe.org</u>

Or scan me instead!

Chapter 52

Surviving the Complicated Adoption Process

"Anyone who welcomes a little child like this on my behalf is welcoming me."
Matthew 18:5

After our initial foray into Cambodia with *Servants,* and also knowing that we would not be able to have more children 'normally' due to previous complications, we decided we would like to adopt. Adopting Sarah was a complicated business (and one which was detailed in Siobhan's biography, *'Dancing in the Light'*). In summary, we decided to adopt in Cambodia whilst we were still in the UK.

We attended a seminar for potential international adopters. They got us to play a 'board game' on the floor with each couple having a piece on the board. We threw the dice and played. Many of the couples did not complete the game and there were many challenges on the way. We realised that the game represented the reality of adoption and the many challenges we faced. Many people do not complete the process of adoption due to these challenges.

We had started the adoption process in the UK before we went to Cambodia with *Tearfund*. After a fairly rigorous process, we were given the OK from social services for an International adoption. One time the social worker came to our house unexpectedly. I was feeding Zoe and Hannah fish fingers and baked beans whilst they were still in the bath. She thought it was hysterical.

When we arrived in Cambodia we needed to settle in rather than start the process then. So it took a while before we were ready. I don't think anything we did before or after compared to the amount of paperwork required for the Cambodian adoption. They did not have a checklist and after we submitted one form another would be required. Months and months it took and Siobhan was required to stop working so she could commit herself to it.

We had heard about Sarah through a Christian orphanage who realised she needed special care and ongoing surgery because of her cleft palate. We wanted her as soon as we saw her. But it took around 18 months to complete the adoption process.

It involved three Ministries that all needed to approve the adoption. The Ministry of Social Affairs, the Ministry of Foreign Affairs, and finally the Senate. We became aware that bribes were being given by some that expedited the process but as a child rights advocate, we didn't think that was something we should do.

Finally, the day came when we could officially receive the necessary paperwork to say that the Adoption was finalised, but we went to the office. We were thrilled. They told us that we could pick up the paperwork the following day. However, when Siobhan went the next day they said that the Government had closed down all international adoptions. The U.S. Embassy had exposed an international baby adoption trafficking ring by Lauren Galida, a Hawaiian woman, so all future adoptions were on hold.

We were anxious that Sarah would be taken away from us but realised that it was internal politics and not about our precious baby Sarah at all, so she remained safe with us. But we could not leave the country until we were allowed to by our embassy.

Over the next few weeks, we realised that there was a dispute between the embassies specifically about our case. The Ministry of Social Affairs said we needed a representative of the Senate to sign off but they said that they had already signed it and therefore lost face. After careful negotiation involving a third party, they finally conceded and we were given the official Cambodian adoption papers. We then paid for them to be translated.

Our paperwork for adoption in the UK had effectively expired as we had taken so long, so we approached the US embassy. They furnished us with more paperwork to complete including psychological profiles by a US-trained Psychologist, but they were not hopeful or in a hurry, so we went back to the British Embassy. They told us that we needed to be in the UK for a year before it could be finalised and provide us with the necessary visa. What a palaver! Nevertheless, we were finally able to officially welcome her into our family.

At one point we went back to the US Embassy. Siobhan had previously provided information to them which resulted in the conviction of an adoption trafficker. They approved Sarah's immigration into the States. Later we went to an immigration meeting in the States for Sarah to obtain citizenship and were told that as I did not have a green card I would be removed from all paperwork, so effectively Siobhan was Sarah's adoptive mother only and I was not her adoptive father. Nevertheless, Sarah did receive an American passport.

It was right for the Royal Government of Cambodia to stop illegal adoptions, but for those of us who had gone through the process legally and carefully, it was very frustrating.

Because I was from the UK we sought help from the British Embassy. We finally got a letter from them saying that we could proceed with the adoption in the UK. After arriving in the UK we had to involve the social services in Swansea City and they then visited us to see that we were providing Sarah with a safe home. After a year we could formalise the adoption in Cardiff High Court and she officially became our daughter to both of us and, subsequently, she was able to hold a British Passport.

The Hague Convention in 1993 developed a series of regulations on how international adoptions should be conducted in order to protect children from being trafficked.

Reflection:

In retrospect we would not recommend people to do international adoptions unless you really understand what you are doing. Children should primarily grow up in their home country if at all possible and international adoptions should be a last resort.

Resource:

- *Hague Convention* on Protection of Children in International Adoption: hcch.net/en/instruments/conventions/full-text/?cid=69

Chapter 53

Surviving 'Losing Face'

"It's when you save face that you have to ask yourself what you are really saving it for."
Anthony T Hincks

When I first went to work with Cambodians in the refugee camp, I visited a barber to trim my beard and tidy up my hair. The cost was much cheaper than back in the UK but I didn't foresee a complication. My lack of language ability meant that I couldn't explain that I wanted a beard trim and not a complete shave. I realised when it was too late. The team said this would likely be my first experience of losing face but certainly not the last. They were right!

Adjusting to living in Cambodia was a series of losing face moments. The main challenge was not to show anger in any way. If you did then the response would be that what you had done was completely unacceptable.

In my role as *Tearfund* representative in Cambodia, I had many wide-ranging responsibilities. A book was published about children. I was eager to read it so I got hold of an English version published in America many years before. I was disturbed by the content which promoted corporal punishment of children. And this, in a post-geno-cidal country! The last thing they needed was an endorse-ment of this brutal form of violence against children.

Violence against children was what my PhD was all about, and I knew how terrible it could be, so I wrote to the Cambodian publisher and told them that it should be taken down. The response was immediate. I don't think any previous book that they had published had ever received any criticism and they "lost face". They were only willing to modify some small sections but left the overall content and structure. I found it deeply upsetting. I wrote to the author who had plans to come to Cambodia but when he came he refused to meet me.

I had the opportunity to go to Japan to the *World Congress on Commercial Sexual Exploitation of Children* in Yokohama. It was a huge event involving U.N., Govern-ment and international NGO leaders from around the world. It was a huge privilege to represent Tearfund.

During that time I was also given an invitation with around 200 other faith NGO leaders to go to Capitol Hill in Washington DC to present the situation on human traf-ficking and sexual exploitation in Cambodia. It was an incredible experience and I could sense just how much political power existed in that place. I met Laura, the Senior Advisor on Human Trafficking, for the *US State Depart-ment* and she said she was coming to Cambodia and asked if I could help to connect her with the faith-based anti-trafficking community there. I was very excited about this and started to arrange for her to meet different NGOs. I knew that the British Ambassador was keen to meet her. He arranged a dinner with all the key UN and NGO Directors.

Reflection:

Sometimes you need to do the right thing, culturally, and other times you need to speak out against injustice, even when it involves taking a risk.

Resource:

- *UN Violence Against Children* research: violenceagainstchildren.un.org/content/un-study-violence-against-children

Chapter 54

Surviving the 'Men in Black'

"Always Remember: The Universe Has A Way Of Leading You To Where You're Supposed To Be, At The Moment You're Supposed To Be There."
Agent High T, Men In Black: International

A s I was making arrangements two 'men in black' suits turned up at our Cambodian wooden house asking why I was making arrangements for her! I explained that she had asked me! Anyway, they changed the hotel arrangements to a more secure one, and I promised to keep them informed. I later had a call from the American Ambassador and he invited himself to the dinner. During the dinner, there was a bit of healthy competition between the ambassadors about what they were doing/supporting, but the outcome was good.

At the end of the visit, Laura the Senior Advisor for the US State Department, suggested that Helen and myself pull together a proposal for a network of faith-based organisations that were working on anti-trafficking. We worked hard with all those involved to put together a proposal and arranged that in the event of receiving the grant the due diligence would be done. After several phone calls in the middle of the night, the outcome of all this was, sadly, that the money was given to already well-established organisations and not our network at all. However, what developed was *Chab Dai* (translated from Cambodian as 'Hands Together') a network of faith-based organisations which grew to over 60 NGOs and proved to be an extraordinarily effective way of transmitting resources and knowledge. It still runs today and I have the privilege of being on the Board.

A group of people came at the same time who were doing a fact-finding mission to set up their organisation *Love 146* in Cambodia. I loved their passion and willingness to do their homework before they started. They invited me to be on their board as someone with field experience. This was to be the organisation that I would work with later on.

Our children learned so much from living in another culture, and we felt that the criticism claiming we had put our children at a disadvantage by living in Cambodia wasn't true at all. They learned so much about life. On one occasion we were in our car and they saw a boy being beaten with a stick by a man at a building site. When the car stopped at the traffic light they leapt out of the car running to help. We had no choice but to pull over and run after them. The man told us that the child had stolen stuff and so he felt he had the right to severely beat the boy who wasn't more than seven years old. When we got the boy to empty his pockets there was nothing in it. We arranged for the boy to get back to his home area. It was a reminder that a terrible rage wasn't far below the surface for people who had little opportunity to process their anger following the genocide.

We didn't have a huge salary but we used what we had to visit families in both the UK and the US in the Summer holidays every other year. *Tearfund* paid for us to go to one location and we paid for the other. We also got to travel around much of Asia in between with our own money. Thailand, Singapore, Malaysia, and later Hong Kong, Laos, and Bali, Indonesia.

On our way to Hong Kong, Siobhan was showing off doing ballet dancing on the moving passenger belt. As she did so she tripped and twisted her ankle. So we had to go back to the check-in and ask them for a wheelchair! They couldn't understand why we didn't need one when we checked in but did now. It was all very embarrassing but we got on the plane and got to Hong Kong. We were staying on one of the islands where some friends said we could use their house but it didn't have cars on the island. So we ended up borrowing a tricycle which was the way people tended to get stuff around the place and used it to transport Siobhan for the rest of the holiday.

Zoe and Hannah attended an international school for missionary kids and we were particularly grateful to some of the early teachers for their knowledge of helping children adjust to their new environment. Later we became concerned about some of the conservative teaching and practices and the children told us that they were disappointed by what they experienced, but that was later.

Reflection:

A genocide has a lasting impact on society, not just on the generation most affected now, but for generations afterwards.

Resource:

- The amazing *Chab Dai* organisation today: chabdai.org

Chapter 55

Surviving My PhD

"It is not that I'm so smart. But I stay with the questions much longer."
Albert Einstein

I started my PhD in the last quarter of the 20th Century. October 1999. I decided to do a PhD mainly because I realised it would give me credibility with Governments, the United Nations and International NGOs, but I really had no idea what it would involve.

I had to attend lectures two days a week for two terms and stay overnight from Sunday to Tuesday. I stayed in a bed and breakfast.

My supervisor, Nigel, said that if I returned to Cambodia to do my fieldwork for my research he was happy for me to keep in touch with him by Zoom and e-mail, and try to meet him in person every year. At one point he came out to Cambodia when we went to a tribal area in Rattinkiri to collect data from children there. We used an MAF plane to get up there and it was great fun. We also swam in a volcanic lake which was amazing!

It was an amazing privilege to do research in every province and see the diversity of the country. The comparative sophistication of Phnom Penh contrasted sharply with the tribal areas in Mondulkiri. In some areas not all the children could write so other children helped them. In the end we did surveys with 1,318 children from every province in addition to focus group work.

The timing for doing the research coincided with the *UN Study on Violence Against Children.* I was able to present my research at a regional meeting. The Government representative was keen to put down the impact of the research findings but was reminded by the chair that until other research superseded it, then it should be considered as the current situation.

Later, I went to speak to UNICEF to persuade them to have a Country-level conference in Cambodia that involved children and adults separately. They said that they would as long as I organised it. It was a huge undertaking. We had a children's conference where representatives from each province had previously met with peers at the provincial level. Each province then developed a banner with a message for the Government on an aspect of violence they were concerned about. For the adult conference, significant UN representatives came from the different agencies (e.g. UNICEF, UNHCR, WHO), as well as NGO representatives and most important of all Royal Government of Cambodian representatives including the Deputy Prime Minister.

In a wonderful breach of protocol, the children were invited to present first so that the senior Government ministers could hear what they had to say. It felt satisfying when I was congratulated by the head of UNICEF for my contribution to making it happen.

Later I was invited to present my research at the Cambodia senate. It was the part on Corporal punishment in school and contributed to decisions from the Ministry of Education to change corporal punishment in schools to be in the law rather than just school policy

In Cambodia I completed the fieldwork required to generate the data for my PhD but I also needed to write it up. I knew there were too many distractions in Cambodia to do that so we decided to come back to the UK. I had also completed my contract with Tearfund so staying would have meant finding another job. We thought we might well come back to Cambodia in the future but at this time we would return to the UK.

Like nearly everyone who does a PhD, I went through different phases. Did I really have the capacity to finish it? (Imposter syndrome). Was it worth it? Was I going to be able to finish it? Did I want to finish it? In the end, I decided it would be worth it because it would give me kudos that would help me do more. I spoke to Siobhan one day about whether I should just give up but she reminded me that it had been difficult for all of the family, NOT JUST ME, and that I WAS going to complete it.

Reflection:

I had no idea when I started my PhD how it would be useful in changing awareness, policy and even the law. I feel that this was God pointing in the direction.

Resource:

- Starting a PhD as an older student: theguardian.com/higher-education-network/blog/2014/jul/25/academics-anonymous-mature-phd-worthless

Chapter 56

Surviving the Bully Landlady

After six years our contract finished with *Tearfund* and we returned to the UK. By then I had collected all the field data needed and wanted to complete my PhD. I went to Swansea to meet with a guy called Chris M who later turned out to effectively be our pastor. I told him I had a day to find somewhere for us to rent. We scanned what was available and chose somewhere in Mumbles which was close to the University and local Hospital. Amazingly, to the surprise of Chris, we found somewhere in Mumbles!

The Welsh are lovely welcoming people and we enjoyed the hospitality of the church, but not everyone was so lovely.

Unfortunately, the landlady turned out to be something

of a bully. The house was full of junk and she never responded to requests we made to move it. We felt constantly nagged and in the wrong.

After a year we decided to leave and she kept all of our deposit saying we had left the place in a mess which was completely untrue. To her, it was about making as much money as possible and as she was a solicitor/lawyer, we had no real chance of successfully appealing. It turned out to be the right thing as with Siobhan's stable job we were able to get a mortgage to buy our own place close to the church.

Siobhan got a job working in a genitourinary medicine (GUM or STI) clinic as the local HIV nurse. I was so proud of her adaptability and ability to work in really tough situations. She couldn't tell me about actual cases because of confidentiality reasons but I know she made a huge difference in people's lives. However, I do think that she saw the worst of people cheating on their partners and that was hard for her.

I continued to do some consultancy work and then got a part-time job with *Viva Network* as their Training Coordinator. Having successfully facilitated the *Celebrating Children* course in Cambodia and co-edited a book with the same name with Dr. Josephine-Joy Wright, they wanted me to work on getting it out to their other networks. Jo-Joy and I did one Training of Trainers in Penang, Malaysia and another in Uganda.

I also helped to write a series of workbooks for organisations to use for local training. Viva changed the name so it was branded by them as *Viva Equip*. In the meantime, more academic versions of the Celebrating Children course, adapted for the context at the Masters level, happened in seminaries in India, the Philippines, and Uganda. But mostly I got my head down to finish writing up my PhD.

Reflection:

We were taken into our landlady's nest but it turned out to be a vipers nest. It may seem insignificant compared to many of the other things described here but it was disappointing and hurtful nonetheless.

Resources:

- *Celebrating Children* book edited by Glenn Miles and Jo-Joy Wright. *Celebrating Children* is to be updated in 2024 to *Celebrating Children Worldwide*: amazon.co.uk/Celebrating-Children-Equipping-children-difficult-circumstances/dp/1842270605.
- CC Workbooks/Viva Equip Workbooks: gmmiles.co.uk

Chapter 57

Surviving a House Fire

"Out of the frying pan into the fire"
(Getting from a bad or difficult situation to a worse one,
often as the result of trying to escape from the bad or
difficult one)
15th Century Fable

When I was a young teenager a house not far from ours burnt to the ground. My mum told me that people had 'rubber necks' and would get in the way of the fireman, but we still went to have a look. It was devastating.

When I worked in the refugee camp there was a huge fire. Most of the refugees had very little but it was heartbreaking to hear that even the few things that they had, including photos and reminders of their past, had been destroyed.

When Sarah was around 7-11 years she would love to

experiment with fire. She found it fascinating to watch the flames.

Siobhan found Sarah sleeping under the bed once when she was about three years old. She lit some candles under the bed and fell asleep. Siobhan could smell smoke and the bed had caught on fire so she dragged Sarah out from under there but Sarah couldn't remember what happened after that because she was so young

And there was another time when Siobhan came into Sarah's bedroom because she said she could smell something and she found she'd been playing with matches. She was rubbing matches along the wall because she figured out you could strike a match by dragging the tip against the walls!

And then the third time was when we were in Wales and she was playing with a candle and tried to see how quickly tissue would burn. It was quick! She dropped it because it burnt her fingers and the carpet caught fire. And she ran out into the hallway and shouted "fire" and Siobhan came in and stomped it out with her shoes.

Reflection:

Sarah did experience attachment challenges where she would test us to the limit to see if we would still be around if she did something that was dangerous or difficult. I had learnt from my own parents who adopted their own child, my sister Belinda, that the key was in communication. Sarah needed to know that we weren't going anywhere, even if we sometimes had to say this through gritted teeth.

Resources:

- Firesetting in children and adolescents: ncbi.nlm.nih.gov/pmc/articles/PMC3859988
- Child Attachment Disorders: patient.info/doctor/child-attachment-disorder-pro

Or scan me instead!

Chapter 58

Surviving Siobhan's Cancer

"You can be a victim of cancer, or a survivor of cancer. It's a mindset."
Dave Pelzer

One time when I was travelling back from a consultancy in India I called Siobhan to have a chat. She had a scan due to some breast lumps but had convinced herself, and me, that they were benign. They were not. The biopsies showed she had breast cancer and it required her to have surgery, chemotherapy, *and* radiotherapy.

We connected with *Maggies,* the local cancer charity but the support from our church was excellent. When she was on steroids she would have surges of energy and dig up the garden removing the remains of a buried dump at the end of the garden. The neighbours thought it was unfair of me not to help her but it was therapeutic for her. At least that is my excuse!

During this time my father also died. I was grateful to be in the same country at the time but was on a bus when I got the news so was unable to get to the hospital until after he had died. He had been such a lovely dad. My brother and I coordinated a memorial service for him. 'A kind gentleman' is on his gravestone.

Between the time I started and the time I finished (2008), it took 9 years to complete my Ph.D. but the time to thoroughly do fieldwork in Cambodia was excellent. In the final years of my PhD I also got a training credential PGCE-PCET at an evening class at *Trinity St. Davids*. Much of my teaching experience was gained overseas in training and conferences but I also did some lecturing at the University.

The children were growing up in Wales and so as the time in the UK drew to an end before we returned to Cambodia, we helped them process what we had enjoyed and looked forward to at a de-briefing (in our case, briefing) centre in Switzerland called *La Rucher*.

Although some consider it foolish for us to return, we felt that we wanted to continue to work in Cambodia. When you are in a situation like this many people change direction to do something they feel is more significant. We felt that the direction we were heading was already significant and didn't want to change it. Siobhan felt strong enough and the oncology clinic was willing to see her infrequently.

At the same time, Siobhan started her own PhD at the *Oxford Centre for Mission Studies*. She had always enjoyed studying and was good at it. The college required her to come to Oxford on a regular basis so she was able to go to the oncology clinic as well as spend the required time in Oxford. She could also visit Zoe who by then had returned to Wales to do her 'A' levels thanks to the kindness of a family in the church who hosted her.

The organisation (Love146) that had come on a fact-finding mission before, contacted me and invited me to be on their board and later to head up their NGO in Cambodia. I was excited but when Siobhan got sick I wondered if they would pull out of needing us. However, they graciously allowed me to continue to work from the UK until we were ready to go.

Reflection:

This time when Siobhan had breast cancer we had to consider the possibility of her dying but we felt that we would have time to talk so we didn't have the really hard conversations. However, we both decided that unless things changed we still felt called back to Cambodia.

Resource:

- Breast cancer in women: <u>nhs.uk/conditions/breast-cancer-in-women</u>

Chapter 59

Surviving India's Largest Residential Area

"Dharavi is a residential area in Mumbai, Maharashtra, India. It is considered India's largest slum and it may have up to a million residents."
Wikipedia

During this time I was able to visit India and return to see the work of a gifted local man called Timothy Gakwad. As well as his work with children his organisation, *IMCares,* also had some clinics in the slum areas. He told me the story of some hijra (transgender) who had come to their women's clinic to ask for help. The staff had to consider whether they were able to help or not but they decided to welcome them. I visited these transgender women in their community and was told that they had been marginalised even by their own community because they had HIV. As we approached their modest slum huts I could see their faces light up as the NGO workers approached. They were, perhaps, the only people

243

who genuinely cared for this exceedingly marginalised community. I was deeply moved.

Later I was able to transfer funds from Love146 so that Timothy could create a docu-drama about the hijra called 'Asha' that could inspire churches to reach out to this deeply marginalised community. On a later visit Jamie from my church accompanied me as the videographer and we made a documentary together to raise awareness in the West about the sexually exploited hijra. We put it on YouTube. I confess that I took it all in my stride but Jamie was deeply moved by the sheer size of the slums and whilst I was impressed with just how organised the slums were his focus was more on the impact of poverty on the many families.

Timothy also introduced me to Jasmir, a flamboyant and deeply compassionate Indian gay man who was the founder of Samabhavana. He told me about his experience doing HIV education for boys and young men in the sex industry that had changed one night when one of the boys contacted him, having been brutally raped to the point he needed surgery on his anus. Jasmir took the boy to hospital for surgery and made sure he was OK. After this event, his emphasis changed to also include addressing alternative employment for boys in the sex industry.

Jasmir took me out one night on the street to where the boys and young men waited to be picked up for sex. Some clinked glass pieces together as they walked through the street to let people know that they were available to massage. They ranged from tiny, skinny boys to big muscular men. I was horrified about one young lad who seemed so young, vulnerable, and fragile. He looked about 9 years old. I asked how long he had been working for and was told around three years. I felt sick. Now I really understood that boys could be just as vulnerable as girls.

We worked together on providing young men with government-approved training, plus soft skills. I got the funds and he did all the hard work with his team. We did a research project before and afterwards to demonstrate the changes that they had experienced. This was one of the first research projects I did with boys, but much of the future research with boys we did drew from our learnings from this project.

I encouraged Jasmir to come and visit and advise us in Cambodia. Even though I had worked for over six years in Cambodia by then I knew very little about the situation of sexual exploitation for young men. The rumour was that it wasn't a problem for boys there. How wrong we were! In a week Jasmir had found several male massage places in Phnom Penh where boys and young men were being sold. My PhD research had shown that boys were sexually abused, but this was a new level.

We followed up with his mapping of where things were and sought to do a research project in the massage parlours with male masseurs. Some of these were hidden around the back streets with or without signs. As we talked to young men and boy masseurs, we would ask them about other locations and that is how we created a map and found out where they were. One place was so exclusive and private that it had cameras around the compound and just standing close to it alerted security guards to come out and enquire about what we were doing. As you can imagine we weren't able to access that place.

Reflection:

Sometimes I am appalled by the greed of the mega-rich and yet I am still in the top wealthiest 1% of the world's population. How am I using my wealth? Timothy's team were reaching out to some of the most vulnerable people on the planet. What am I doing to reach out to the vulnerable in my community?

Resources:

- The video made by Jamie Sampson and I: *Life of a Hijra: Accepted or Rejected?* youtu.be/ _m9aZ1nJvUA

Or scan me instead!

- Samabhavana - dignity in life: samabhavana.in

Chapter 60

Surviving being Robbed in Cambodia

"Ordinary riches can be stolen; real riches cannot. In your soul are infinitely precious things that cannot be taken from you."
Oscar Wilde

W hen we went to live in Cambodia as a family for the first time we lived in a simple Cambodian wooden house. It was much better than the slum, but still fairly basic. We quickly learned that it was important to have a security guard even though we had barbed wire around the fences. We were told that people would assume we had something worth stealing even though we didn't. We inherited our first night guard from the previous Scottish family who lived in the house. But if we went out in the evening he would often be fast asleep when we returned. We realised he would be unlikely to do much even if he was awake.

We had to move to our second house when the Prime Minister's sister turned up with a military escort saying that she wanted to bulldoze our house and build flats in its place. Our landlord had disappeared in the night and our neighbour on the other side also had to leave. We were given two weeks to leave and find somewhere else.

At one point we had a burglary in our office, which was under our house, by someone who we are convinced was trying to retrieve photos we had of children being tied to their beds in the orphanage scam described before. He didn't get anything because by that stage we had a real night guard with a machete (!) but it was unsettling for us as a family.

Returning to Cambodia for the second time was exciting and we were pleased to reconnect with friends. One expatriate couple, Nigel and Millet, who we had known from before told us about a wooden house they had available for rent, so we moved in. We loved the house itself but sadly, in the first week, we were robbed. Although we had bars on the windows they cleverly used hooks and wires to pull things through the bars. We lost our laptops and phones. What a welcome back to Cambodia!

I really enjoyed working with *Love146* developing partnerships and doing research in the region. One thing I particularly enjoyed was working with interns who came to work for three months to a year. For some it was their first experience of working overseas or being involved in justice work and I would support them, often in groups of 3-5, to work on a specific research project. As a result we were able to understand the situation of sexually exploited women, men, transgender and children. The learning was designing the research, conducting it, analysing it, writing it up and presenting it. Later on many of these projects got written into peer review journals and gave something concrete to the participants that they could put into their CVs.

Reflection:

Possessions are not important but someone getting into your house is deeply disturbing. It's an invasion of your personal space.

Resource:

- How to deter burglars: theecoexperts.co.uk/home-security/deter-burglars

Chapter 61

Surviving the Ten year Longitudinal Research Project

"There is nothing in a caterpillar that tells you it's going to be a butterfly."
R. Buckminster Fuller

My new role in Cambodia with *Love146*, the Anti-trafficking organisation I was working for, was to do capacity building of those organisations who had little resources to do what they were doing better. By then *Chab Dai* was well established as a networking organisation and supported around 60 organisations. Helen spoke to us and asked if Siobhan could be the project manager for a ten-year longitudinal research project. This was an incredible idea to follow survivors of sex trafficking and listen to their stories of restoration even after and well into the time they had completed the initial residential care. Rehabilitation in the community was as important, if not more important, than the initial residential care.

Trying to access funding for a ten-year endeavour was

unlikely to be considered by a University, never mind an NGO. Some said it would never happen. Even funding in 3-year cycles was difficult, but Helen had faith that it was going to happen and with her extraordinary commitment, it did.

Once the project was established then the organisations that were once reluctant at the beginning wanted to be involved. It took around two years to get all the memorandums of understanding signed by all the organisations involved. Helen and Siobhan were both charismatic and persuasive. Whilst Helen found funders, Siobhan got the organisations and participants involved. One of the challenges was to get participants who were genuinely trafficked. Some organisations took in girls who were vulnerable to being trafficked rather than actually trafficked.

I worked with Siobhan on developing a methodology but the first year was about gaining the trust of organisations that had shelter and community-based programs to be able to interview the survivors and sign agreements. This was more complicated than we thought it was going to be. By the end of the year, Siobhan had signed up 14 organisations and 128 participants. It was named the Butterfly Longitudinal Research Project.

Over the years we produced annual reports and updates on research findings. After several years we focused on thematic reports that analysed data on specific topics, including sexual exploitation of boys and the impact of faith on recovery. Some of the findings could be immediately applied to the shelters to improve care, such as the exposure of sexual harassment between clients in shelters leading to better child safeguarding policies and procedures.

In 2021, I contacted the editor of *Dignity,* an open access peer review journal that focuses on Violence and

Exploitation, and asked if they would consider doing a special issue focusing on the Butterfly project. James, who was supporting the Butterfly project at the time agreed and we worked together with authors to submit eight articles to be peer-reviewed. It was a long arduous process but by the end of the year, we had eight papers published.

Reflection:

I am so proud of Siobhan's achievement in launching the inaugural flight of the Butterfly. The Butterfly Project continues to impact anti-trafficking efforts around the world.

Resources:

- *The Butterfly Project* peer review papers: digitalcommons.uri.edu/dignity/vol6/iss4.

Or scan me instead!

- Other researchers have worked on other papers as well. The rest are listed here: chabdai.org/butterfly

Chapter 62

Surviving the Red Light Districts of South East Asia

"Red is such an interesting colour to correlate with emotion, because it's on both ends of the spectrum. On one end you have happiness, falling in love, infatuation with someone, passion, all that. On the other end, you've got obsession, jealousy, danger, fear, anger and frustration."
Taylor Swift

One time when I was teaching the Master's course in Holistic Child Development at *Asia Pacific Nazarene Theological Seminary* I met an enthusiastic guy called Jarrett who shared interests with me. He was hoping to do a PhD. We stayed in touch and although he didn't get into a paid PhD program he offered to come and work as an intern for me. I was delighted for him to join me. He made arrangements and shortly after arriving said he needed to speak to me privately. He admitted that he had recently come out as a gay man to his parents just before he came to Cambodia.

I could see he was tense and it became apparent that he thought that I might ask him to pack his bags to leave. Bless him! I said that it was fine and that could we talk about the research now! I could see the sense of relief on his face but it was a sad situation that a talented young man could think that he could not work with a faith-inspired organisation because he admitted to being gay. I still work with Jarrett 13 years later. We are on Zoom calls 3-4 times a week. He hasn't got his Ph.D. yet but he has gained a reputation as an excellent researcher. He is happily married to his husband and living in New York.

As we gained a reputation, several other young people, some graduate and undergraduate students from around the world, volunteered to work with us. This was fantastic and enabled us to do a range of research projects that we wouldn't otherwise have been able to do. We did research in Phnom Penh with women in the massage parlours (another group who were largely neglected by NGOs) and street children, in Siem Reap in Cambodia with boys in the massage industry, Chiang Mai, Thailand with boys in the sex industry and street children and in Manila, the Philippines with young men in the sex industry and street children.

Jarrett spoke Tagalog language and we decided to do research in Manila firstly with men in the sex industry and later with street children. We went to one area which was the remnants of a previous US army base left over from Vietnam war-times. We went together into this dense area and must have looked overwhelmed by the extent of what was going on. An expat who appeared to live there assumed we were lost and needed direction so he mapped out where to find the various 'sex' services'. We thanked him but all we could think of was about the people who were being exploited. It was very disturbing.

One time I took a group of students from the Seminary to visit a brothel in Manila's red-light area. As we sat down the men brought us a lineup of around ten young women. We invited three of them to sit down with us and have a drink so we could talk to them. As we watched what was going on around us we realised that women selected were being taken to a side room for sexual services. It was a no-win situation. If you were 'chosen' you were sexually exploited. If you were not chosen you were not paid and forced to quit, leaving you to find another equally difficult way to earn money.

Later when I was staying in a hotel there was a knock on the door at around 3am from a woman asking if I wanted a massage. I was frustrated and sad that this woman knew that I, as a man, was on my own. She had clearly been told by the staff at the front desk. I complained to the manager but of course there was no follow-up. We did actually offer to do training in the hotel for the staff to be aware of people trafficking (!) but they would not admit that they were at fault. I have been impressed by some hotels in Asia that are strict and have signs at the front desk with regulations about having visitors in guest rooms.

We did research with a sexually exploited transgender in Bangkok. Although Bangkok has a reputation among foreigners for being very 'lady-boy' friendly, and you certainly see a lot more freedom than in Phnom Penh, the reality we found in our research was that they still deal with regular discrimination and violence. After the fun and glitter of the 'lady-boy' shows many of the showgirls experienced being stalked and raped, and even gang raped. That is the part the punters/sex buyers and tourists don't see or want to see or are even aware of.

In Bangkok, I met Celeste who had a ministry to reach out to ladyboys in Soi Nana, the epicentre for sex tourism. She took them cookies and chatted with them in Thai and they clearly loved her. The ladyboys looked fabulous in their outfits but it wasn't until I reflected on my visit that I realised they were all much the same size. They would do pole dancing dressed in polka-dot bikinis or nurse's uniforms but their shape and size were identical; slim, shapely with large breasts. Fat, short, or older transgender were noticeable by their absence. We learned that many took 'the pill' for feminisation, had surgery, and injected their own faces to maintain their appearance and, of course, all this was risky without proper medical supervision. When their looks disintegrated they were quickly dispensed with.

We visited one brothel in the heart of Bangkok that was catering for Muslim men. The women were all chubby which was the preferred type and ironically had veils over their faces. It was sad to see yet another form of exploitation.

Thailand is the regionally largest sex tourism destination in Southeast Asia. A study by a Thai university estimated the sex sector at **around $25 billion**, or 12% of the country's gross domestic product.

Reflection:

Governments have to choose what they are going to do about sex tourism. Do they promote it, discourage it, or turn a blind eye? What are the moral consequences of allowing it to continue?

Resources:

- Research we did into the sexual exploitation of boys and men in Thailand: <u>No Other Choice: A Baseline Study on the Vulnerabilities of Males in the Sex Trade in Chiang Mai, Thailand</u>

Or scan me instead!

- Economics of sex tourism in Thailand <u>medium. com/@lovinalilian/the-profit-of-exploitation-sex-tourism-and-the-use-of-bodies-in-thailand-e960cb739416</u>

Chapter 63

Surviving a Typhoon in Manila

"Hurricane season brings a humbling reminder that, despite our technologies, most of nature remains unpredictable."
Diane Ackerman

When I was at All Nations Christian College in 1987 there was a huge storm. It was one of the biggest storms that the UK had experienced in a hundred years. In an old house like we were in you could hear the wind coming through every nook and cranny. But we were all shocked in the morning to hear the devastation it had caused throughout the UK. Even in the grounds of the College many old trees had blown over. But this was nothing compared to my experience in the Philippines.

I helped Love146, the organisation I was with, to recruit Dr. Gundelina, a Psychologist who was working in the Philippines. She was a gold mine and ran a shelter in Manila for girls and later boy survivors of sex trafficking.

She had the vision of a round shelter where no one could get lost in a corner. Love 146 helped her to fulfil her dream.

One time she invited me to come to teach a class in Manila and set me up in a building outside of the city. We had around 20 students from around Asia, some local and some expats. One morning I was teaching and was getting stuck into my topic when one of the students stopped me. "Dr. Miles, there's a hurricane!". It was only then that I noticed that there was indeed a hurricane happening outside the window. We were in a wooden/bamboo structure and doing a quick risk assessment I decided it might be safer for us to move to the concrete building where the students were sleeping, but getting there was going to be a problem.

I encouraged the group to gather their stuff and keep together. But as we moved out of the building we noticed serious debris flying around including large sheets of corrugated iron wrapping itself around the tree. In addition to that, there was also mud sliding off the hills next to the camp area. The mud pushed over the stone wall and came pouring into the compound.

It taught me how different people respond to being in a crisis. Some were scared and others were excited. I didn't appreciate the latter when it was so dangerous but of course some took videos on their phone which proved to others that it really had been as alarming as we had said.

We made it over to the concrete building which was fortunately two stories high so we could head to the upper story. The rain and mud poured into the area downstairs and all we could do was wait and pray wondering if the roof of that building would remain secure. Of course, most of us knew nothing of hurricanes/tornadoes but when things calmed down there was a huge mess everywhere and we were effectively cut off as all wifi was down.

We heard later that some billboards had come loose on the highway and several people had been killed. My phone was one of the few phones at the time that was able to connect with the outside world so everyone used it to tell their family they were safe when, sadly, the news had not reached outside of the Philippines!

Typhoon Yolanda, internationally known as Haiyan, is the deadliest typhoon to have affected the country in recorded history, killing more than 6,300 people as it crossed the Visayas region in November 2013.

Reflection:

One of the worst natural hazards that affects increasing numbers of people is hurricanes/typhoons. Although on the news we hear about those in the States, we hear very little about those in Asia and the devastating impact they have on people.

Resources:

- Significant natural hazards in the Philippines: reliefweb.int/report/philippines/philippines-2023-significant-natural-hazards-and-conflicts-snapshot-12-january-2024
- Safety Tips before, during and after a Hurricane: constellation.com/energy-101/hurricane-safety-tips.html

Chapter 64

Surviving Working in Cambodia's Red Light Districts

"The most beautiful thing in Cambodia isn't the country - it's the Cambodian people."
Rithy Panh

P roviding support for survivors of trafficking was one thing but I wanted to explore ways to challenge the demand side of trafficking. I heard about a guy in Bangkok who was working with *YWAM* conducting a project called the *MST* (*Men and the Sex Trade*) project. It was reaching out to expatriate men in the red light areas and challenging them. I immediately liked Chris and I thought his idea was brilliant. I invited him to come to Cambodia to do training for expat Christian men there. One of the guys who attended that first meeting was John, a Republican from the States. We couldn't have been more different but we both had a passion to reach out to the men. We later broke off from the MST project in Bangkok and named our organisation the *GLUE* project. *The Guys*

Like Us Education project was similar to *MST* but different in that I believe we allowed a bit more grace for men who wanted to go out with us.

So the idea was to meet for a time of worship and prayer followed by a time on the street. When we first started we used a survey to make contact with the men asking them questions about why they were there and what they thought about the sex industry. It was mainly to engage with them. We ended up doing this every other Friday evening. At first, we were out until 3 am but we realised that most men were too drunk to have a decent conversation after midnight so we agreed to end at midnight. My family was happier too as I was less likely to be grumpy on Saturday! We dispensed with the survey and just connected with people directly by asking them how they were and starting a conversation.

In many ways, it was the hardest project to evaluate because a guy you engaged in a conversation with might be deeply impacted and at the same time another guy could get angry with us. Another might appear to be listening but then head off to a brothel. But we felt it was the right thing to do and I learned a lot about the way these guys justified what they were doing. One guy explained to me that HE was the one being exploited. He had paid a girl money to stay with only him and then she had gone off with another guy. He couldn't see the incongruity of it. Other guys believed that it was a simple exchange. *"She needs money. I need sex",* but they missed the huge power differential which meant that he had all the choices and she had no real choice.

One guy I spoke with who was a guard at the American Embassy was out drinking with his mates but chose to have a chat. He told me that he had worked in different parts of the world. If he met a woman in a hotel bar in London and wanted to have sex with her he felt that the power difference between them was much smaller than the same scenario in Phnom Penh, and this prevented him from using women in Cambodia. I wish I had recorded him saying this. He understood in a way most men didn't about those power differences. He may not have known it, but he was a big muscular male feminist! I was proud of him.

We developed a reputation among certain quarters and even got written up in the expat online platform for expat men who were in Cambodia to buy sex! One night when we were out a man got his camera out to take photos of us. When I refused he asked me if I was "ashamed of being a Christian?". I responded that I wasn't but just didn't want my photo taken, thank you! Many men knew we were Christian and sometimes we would get the middle finger but most ignored us or just let us get on with it. It was a huge learning experience for me. Although I was/am aware that some men were brutal sadists, many were lonely, sad men who believed that change for themselves wasn't possible. They justified themselves that they weren't doing any harm but 'helping the girls'. Although most people wouldn't bother with them, we knew that if we changed the heart of one man then it might make a big impact and prevent many girls and boys from being abused.

I developed a friendship with one expat guy called Steve (!) in the red light area who was a troubled soul. He told me that as a young man, he had been sexually exploited in the UK by a group of older women. He longed to do the right thing but became increasingly manipulative in getting money for his drug habit. I and many others tried to help him and it took a long time for me and others to let go and realise I was doing more harm than good. He also started an unhelpful rumour about me so I felt it was time to say goodbye.

One day a friend invited me to come and see a market area that was converted into a bar area. They were renting out the plots. He suggested that we could rent a plot and use it as a place where women in the area could find a safe space. We decided to call it a tongue-in-cheek name called the '*Message Parlour*'. Yes, you heard it right. Not massage. It was about the size of a small one-car garage but had enough space for a couch, a freezer and a water dispenser. The freezer contained ice cream to sell so it at least looked like a legitimate enterprise!

Later we got the plot next door and it became a colourful gated safe space for children of women in the sex business with cartoon videos, beanbags, and toys. Our staff would sit with them and read storybooks. Most of the bar owners were really pleased to see a place where children could be safe. Most people frequenting the area didn't like to think children were being exploited. Many men told us that they would never hurt a child, they only sought sex with women (or men) but what they didn't realise was that most of the people who were in the sex industry in Cambodia had started work when they were around 14 years old, shortly after puberty, and some, though fewer, a lot earlier than that.

Sadly the cost of having these two projects side by side increased dramatically and we were unable to continue.

Research we did with street children found that the majority of streets involved boys and young men who were sexually exploited.

As we did research with young men and boys in Cambodia working in the sex industry, we came across several transgender women and realised that apart from

HIV education they received very little attention from the anti-trafficking movement. We did research late at night/early in the morning in places we heard that they 'worked'. We saw first-hand the way one was brutally kicked by the police and how they said they were "treated like dogs" as one described to us. Most of the research we did on sexual exploitation was in collaboration with NGOs who were doing something to address the issue but there was no one working with this very vulnerable group. One time a transgender woman got off the back of a motorbike carrying a brick. She said it was insurance 'in case the client got violent'. One of the saddest comments from one was that they did this work because it was the only opportunity for them to have sex (and feel love) with a 'real' man. In reality, they were being used and there was no safe place for them to experience love or even a bit of kindness, apart from each other.

Reflection:

I have sometimes been criticised as an academic that I am away from real life, but working in the Message Parlour and with the GLU project helped me to see it first hand.

Resources:

- *The MST Project* based in Bangkok: themstproject.com
- Research we did with Phnom Penh's street-involved children digitalcommons.uri.edu/dignity/vol6/iss1/6

Or scan me instead!

- Research we did with transgender/ladyboys: digitalcommons.uri.edu/dignity/vol3/iss2/1

Glenn Miles PhD

Or scan me instead!

Chapter 65

Surviving Angry Perpetrators

'The elephant that is stuck in the mud will take down the tree with it."
Cambodian Proverb

One day an expat German guy turned up for a chat and trailing behind him was a young shy Cambodian girl. I asked my staff to check if the girl (aged around 14 years old) was OK and she would not admit to anything, so we couldn't do anything. But a few days later the girl turned up at the *Message Parlour* and told us she was being raped and wanted to get out. The staff called me and we went into action. We got the girl to a safe shelter.

We referred the perpetrator to our colleagues at *International Justice Mission* and they worked with the authorities to make sure he went to jail. IJM is an organisation that, in contrast to most anti-trafficking organisations which are mostly female-run, was run by mainly police and lawyers who are predominantly men. It required a different approach to communicate with them. Initially, they were only about the rescue but over time realised that rescue requires long-term consideration.

So the man was arrested and ended up in jail. After he had been in jail for about 18 months he was released. In theory, he should have been driven straight to the airport but he ended up back in the red light area looking for me. The staff informed me and I went over immediately to protect them, although I was pretty scared to be honest. He spent over an hour telling me that I was a terrible Christian and how he had lost part of his life due to me. I let him shout and scream for a while and then gently asked him to leave. At one point he said, "I did f*** her", and I reminded him that this was why he went to jail and not due to what I did or did not do.

Wendy lived in Wales and a friend told her about what we were doing. She felt a very strong calling to join us so she contacted me and told me God had told her to come and work with me in the red light area. It was actually before the *Message Parlour* was started and I told her I didn't really have a suitable position for her but I told her about other organisations she could contact.

When the *Message Parlour* started to take shape I remembered what she had said and contacted her. I asked her if she had found anything else and she said she hadn't because she was waiting until something came up where she could work directly with me. God had told her so. She ended up being a huge asset to us and her 'complicated' background gave her the ability to talk to both girls and pundits in a relaxed and non-threatening manner.

Virgins were premium and cost the punter/sex buyer US$1000 or more a time and this dropped to a few dollars after they lost their virginity. Most punters were Asian businessmen. Once they had been 'broken in' the price of the girls dropped considerably. The IJM organisation did an undercover video of what they saw and the video was distributed to many news outlets around the world. The video showed young children offering sex to an expatriate man.

Understandably many people were horrified by what they saw and this led to a large number of organisations and individuals heading to Cambodia. Many were convinced God had called them there. Some organisations knew what they were doing but some were not qualified. Most of them assumed that they would be able to find and rescue hundreds of girls. They had not considered that boys and young men, women over 18 years, and transgender who also needed help. As a result, many shelters were set up with vulnerable girls but not necessarily those who had been exploited. Some took in girls who were 'at risk' (who they then became a different kind of risk). But then you had the same problem every orphanage has of institutionalisation and the potential of abuse within the shelter. We needed people to consider community-based solutions.

One research project we did in Chiang Mai, Thailand, we invited academics from the local university, NGO staff, the press, and the US Trafficking in Persons office staff. After presenting for an hour we were delighted when people stayed behind to ask questions of us and the social work staff for an additional hour. After a few weeks we had responses from a number of people, including a paedophile who tried to persuade us that it wasn't as we had said but that the boys enjoyed it. We had proof from the boys that this was simply not true. We were disturbed to receive this feedback but glad of the wide reach we received.

I am keen that we address the issue of paedophiles being rehabilitated and helped rather than simply punished. Of course, they need to face the consequences of harming children but isolation is not the answer. I am impressed with the *Mennonite Central Committee Circles* program that seeks to provide a community for sex offenders when they leave jail.

When I was in Wales a mother called me to ask for my help. Her son was arrested for looking at child porn. She had previously been involved in mission work and could find no help from the church. She told me he had been looking at adult porn and had come across child porn and chose to report it. I told her that I wasn't a psychologist so did not know if I could help. After that she became angry and said that no one in the church was willing to help. I agreed to meet him on several occasions and just met him to be a listener. I don't know if it helped but I hope so.

Reflection:

Confronting the perpetrator was not easy. I hate confrontations. But it needed to be done. This seems to be an increasing pattern for me; to confront injustice.

Resources:

- *International Justice Mission* tackling sexual violence through prosection: ijm.org/our-work/violence-women-children/sexual-violence
- *Mennonite Central Committee*: Circles of Accountability to help paedophiles leaving prison: mcc.org/opportunity/circles-support-and-accountability-cosa-alberta

Or scan me instead!

Chapter 66

Surviving Competition Rather than Collaboration

"A bunch of sticks cannot be broken"
Cambodian Proverb

Working with *Chab Dai* was all about collaboration and learning, but as resources were limited, some organisations became more competitive for the limited funds available.

Chab Dai provided education and support to every faith-based organisation that wanted it (who were seeking to address human trafficking in Cambodia). Heads of these small organisations were able to draw on the experience of existing organisations and learn from them. People were mostly learning on the job, even those with experience and training, so people were open to learning. Over time the emphasis went from focusing on rescue to rehabilitation to reintegration. In the beginning, some organisations only wanted to rescue but unless you had somewhere for them to go this wasn't helpful. Others were happy to provide shelter but couldn't always see that this only needed to be temporary and it was best if the women could go home, if safe. Thankfully this has changed somewhat over time but there is still more needed to consider how to do better prevention.

One project that we developed with *Chab Dai* was large flip books for teaching children about sexual abuse and exploitation called the *'Good Touch Bad Touch flipbooks'*. It was a simple story about three children who learned some key messages at school to protect themselves but then on the way home met Uncle Cool. The story was transferable to many other contexts and didn't need electricity to use it. It was subsequently translated into Thai, Vietnamese, Tagalog, and Cebuano, and then a Nepali cartoon version was created which could be used in South Asia including India, Bangladesh, and Pakistan. Later it was picked up by Sam and Hannah in Zambia, Africa, and adapted and used in Uganda and other African nations. Also, another version was developed for Mali and other Muslim countries in Africa (see Surviving resources).

Another prevention tool in the form of a flipbook was created and called *Youth Against Porn*. It was a story about a boy who becomes unhelpfully 'addicted' to porn and in the process he receives some healing. It also contains a sub-story where a girl is at risk of being videoed for porn. Again it contains key messages to be learnt. These flip books have been popular and so we are in the process of developing others that address Bullying, Period Poverty and Grooming for Trafficking.

I attended a conference at *Fuller Seminary* in California on Human Trafficking and was keen for there to be outcomes rather than raising awareness about the issue of human trafficking. We needed to get past raising awareness about the issue. Most people who attended were already aware of the issue and I felt that we needed to explore how we could develop a Christian foundation for the work that faith-based organisations were doing. It was clear that a predominantly higher number of Christian organisations were involved in this issue and yet I felt that there hadn't been enough work convincing us that God was behind our work supporting these very vulnerable people. So we had a small meeting of people who were willing to write and create the outline of an edited volume called '*Stopping the Traffick*'. One of the people was Christa who is a leading expert in anti-trafficking

It was a lot of work but three years later Christa and I were presenting the finished result at the *International Christian Alliance addressing Prostitution* (ICAP) in Green Lake, Wisconsin, USA. We have subsequently, over 12 years, been involved in doing two other edited volumes. It has been a labour of love (and sometimes frustration) but the chapters are an amazing collection of stories and insights from academics, theologians and practitioners from around the world. Two follow-up edited volumes were later developed (see resources).

Living in a society that is primarily capitalistic means that profit is more important than people and slavery is part of the chain of supply and demand. We demand cheap products but these products are often made by people who are effectively modern-day slaves. I wrote to *Cadbury's* several years ago to remind them to go back to their roots and treat their employees fairly in the cocoa farms. They responded years later saying that they were then Fairtrade. However I understand that new ownership may have changed this.

In Cambodia, there is an artist, Stef, who paints *'Happy Cambodia'*. His selection included pictures of happy girls outside a brothel. I wrote to him to say how much I enjoyed seeing his pictures and had even brought some but I was not happy with those particular pictures. I asked friends to also write to him and he took them down!

Reflection:

I admit that I am a high achiever but my intention is that I can achieve a lot for humanity. I get disappointed when I feel that I have had an unproductive day, week, month or year, but I am glad when things come together even if it takes a long time and sometimes it does.

Resources:

- Glenn Miles and Christa Foster Crawford Editors of:

1. *Stopping the Traffick: A Christian Response to Sexual Exploitation & Trafficking* (Regnum 2014)
2. *Finding Our Way Through the Traffic: Navigating our way through the complexities of a Christian response to sexual exploitation and Human Trafficking* (Regnum 2017).
3. *Stepping out of the Traffick: Pausing for Theological Reflection; A Christian response to sexual exploitation and trafficking* (Regnum 2024)
4. All are available from ocms.ac.uk/regnum and *Amazon* in paperback and ebook versions.

Or scan me instead!

- *Fairtrade -* fairtrade.org.uk

Chapter 67

Surviving Dog Bites from Two Cambodian Dogs

"The average dog is a nicer person than the average person."
Andy Rooney

One of the first things Siobhan had to do when she started working in the refugee camp was to find a dog who had bitten someone, arrange to have its head removed and then send it to the lab to see if it had rabies. Welcome to Site 2!

On my way out one day in Phnom Penh a gate opened automatically to allow a car in and two Alsatians leaped out and started chewing my leg. I was rather alarmed but the driver managed to call them and secure them, before telling me he was a doctor and if I came inside the house to his private clinic he could dress the wounds and give me a tetanus jab which I did. I followed up with Gloria, the Australian medic and she said there hadn't been rabies in Phnom Penh for over a decade so it was highly unlikely I would get it. I trusted her advice even though there were a huge number of bats in the city.

Over the years our house became a menagerie with various pets over the years including Bobby the dog, rabbits, guinea-pigs, two scrawny kittens found in the market that became our cats, koi fish in the pond, other tropical fish in a tank, budgerigars and a parrot. The children had names for all and we loved them all. In fact the first day we arrived in Cambodia with the children Zoe and Hannah told our Cambodian friend that they needed a dog. They remembered that I had said at some point we might consider having a dog when we got to Cambodia. There wasn't much negotiation and by the end of the week, Bobby was part of the family. He was a lovely dog and we all loved him.

Similarly, we had interns of all shapes and sizes. Mostly they were wonderful and I think they learned a massive amount in their time with us, but one person turned out to be completely loopy. Our first impression was much the same as the others. Pleasant and keen. We had told all the interns that when they came they would have responsibilities and that we were kind of dependent on them to do their job. This made it much more interesting than the kind of jobs most interns have where it wouldn't matter if they weren't there. Most of them really enjoyed this except for one intern who turned out to cause a massive headache.

I had 'lent' her to Siobhan to work on the Butterfly project. Siobhan checked on her and asked her for drafts but she kept saying it was coming. The problem is that it wasn't. The day which she knew was the final day for needing to send the report to the donor came and Siobhan went to her and found that she had done virtually nothing at all. And in addition to that she blamed us. Poor Siobhan was left to deal with her hissy fit, explaining to the donor and trying to complete the report. Awful. In addition, I had to confront her which I hate.

We had to move on several occasions for all sorts of reasons but we were pleased to move to a large wooden house that had a beautiful garden. The only downside was that it was next to a very stinky canal which not infrequently wafted into our compound, but we had a gazebo where we were able to hold small meetings and one couple asked if they could have their wedding in our garden! We also had a great birthday party there for my 50th. Bobby took guarding the perimeter very seriously. Sadly, the owners asked us to leave because they were selling the land to developers. Later we saw eight very ordinary petya laveng (houses) replace our own beautiful wooden house but we could not complain as it helped provide homes for eight families rather than one.

Reflection:

I was actually quite embarrassed to live in such a beautiful house because I knew others didn't have such a lovely place to live. But my daughter Zoe and friend Meri encouraged me to just enjoy it whilst we had it and they were right.

Resource:

- What to do if you are bitten by a dog: cdc.gov/rabies/specific_-groups/veterinarians/person_bitten.html

Chapter 68

Surviving being 'Let Go' (Fired) in Cambodia

"When I let go of what I am, I become what I might be."
Lao Tzu

I t wasn't an easy relationship with the home office of Love
146, the anti-trafficking organisation I was a part of, but I
thought I was mostly doing OK. We had achieved so
much of what I thought was required in terms of networking
and supporting projects. I was doing capacity building on
many levels. Then one day a friend came to me. She was on the
board of another organisation and she said how excited she was
about the possible merger with their organisation in Cambodia.
I thought I had misheard as I knew nothing about it.

Then, after many requests from me asking them to
come and visit what we were doing in Cambodia, the CEO
and President came to visit. Just before they left I asked
them what they thought. They said they were impressed by
all that was happening, including the large team of volun-

teer interns, but what I had not realised was that they had come to have secret meetings with another organisation that they had told me nothing about.

When they told me several weeks later that they had plans to merge with an established organisation I then realised what the friend had meant. They told me that it was essential that I did not talk about it with anyone. I could see the advantages and disadvantages of a merger but I felt hurt that I wasn't involved at all in the discussions. At the time I was good friends with (another) Steve (P), the Director of the potential merger organisation, and we were in the ridiculous situation of not being able to talk about the merger when we had lunch together. Furthermore, I later heard that he would be the new Director. My role was unknown. That was really hurtful. What had I done wrong?

And this is where I made the mistake of talking to a member of the board of the other organisation, Graham. Graham had also been the pastor at the International church I was a part of. I told him some of my frustrations.

I was invited to meet with the CEO and President of Love 146 in Vietnam when they were in meetings about the merger. When they met me they told me that they were deeply upset that I had spoken to Graham. They had spoken to him and he had told them what I had said (I later found out that this had not happened. He had simply told them that it was inappropriate for him to share what we had talked about in a pastoral meeting.) But at the time I felt so guilty for speaking to him. I wept for being so foolish even though it had not affected the outcomes of the merger decisions at all. The board of the potential merging organisation had decided independently without my input that they were not going to merge based on a lack of responses to crucial questions.

A few weeks later the Chair of the Board spoke to me on a Zoom call to say that I was to be "let go", or fired and that they would come to Cambodia to close everything down within weeks. I asked to speak to the board but they refused.

I felt sick to the stomach. I prepared a speech to give them, but they had already made up their minds. It dawned on me over time and in discussions with others that I actually hadn't done anything wrong. They did provide reasonable financial packages for Cambodian staff who had to leave but I was sick that everything we had invested in for years had to stop within a few weeks, not even six months or so to complete projects. One intern had only recently arrived and they had to turn around and go home. It was around November and my daughter Hannah needed to complete her International Baccalaureate so we needed to stay in Cambodia until the following June. My salary ended at the end of the year.

At that time my body 'held the score' (see resource). I lost a lot of weight, got sicker and struggled with excessive fatigue. I also started coughing badly. Although we would have liked to stay in Cambodia we decided after Hannah finished her schooling it was probably better to go home.

I was in meetings in the UK in April and stopped by at our church in Swansea. One of the church leadership team was a surgeon, Tim, and he managed to arrange for me to have a biopsy by him as there was suspicion of lymphoma. It turned out to be the auto-immune disease sarcoidosis, so not cancer, but still debilitating. It confirmed to us we should come home. As I work in the social justice space I realise more and more how many people working in intense situations become seriously sick after a particular personal or work crisis.

After we returned to the UK we were very happy to return to Linden, the church we had previously been a part of in Swansea. They were very caring and we quickly rebuilt friendships there. Siobhan managed to get a job working in a residential centre for people with long-term chronic conditions. She also stayed in touch with her colleagues/friends doing the Butterfly Research project in Cambodia.

By then I had a large network of contacts in organisations around the world involved in human trafficking. My energy was limited but I still managed to be involved in supporting a number of projects. I especially stayed in touch with Jarrett who remained in Cambodia and then later moved to New York with his partner Paul who later became his husband. We continued to work on a range of projects and he independently became a renowned expert.

Reflection:

Being fired was extremely painful and traumatic. I realised that I defined myself by my work and that was not helpful. I lost weight. I got sick. And it didn't just affect me, it impacted the children and Siobhan too because we were all in it together. A very hard time.

Resources:

- *The Body Keeps the Score*: <u>youtube.com/watch?v=QSCXyYuT2rE</u>
- Survive being fired: <u>builtin.com/articles/survive-being-fired</u>

Chapter 69

Surviving Chronic Auto-immune Disease

"When sick, you take the elephant to pray. When you are better, you offer a chicken egg."
Cambodian Proverb

I t's not easy to wake up every morning in pain. It's also not really considered appropriate for me to talk about being in pain. I recently had a cystoscopy and the doctor laughed when I said, "Ouch that really hurt!". Men are expected to, "take it like a man".

An autoimmune disorder occurs when the body's immune system attacks and destroys healthy body tissue by mistake. After being fired I was diagnosed with sarcoidosis.

Sarcoidosis is primarily a lung disease but apart from a bad cough, my main challenge has been more the fatigue that went with it, similar to M.E (Myalgic Encephalomyelitis). It initially left me sleeping much of the day. Something I found helpful was the 10-bottle toolkit. This means that you have ten bottles of energy a day. If you overdo it you don't have enough bottles the next day so have to reduce them. It has helped me to pace myself a bit better although my natural tendency is still to overdo it, especially if I am working on a project I am passionate about.

In addition to this, I have had other challenges. I have had dry patches of psoriasis since puberty in my scalp, arms and groyne. Sometimes it is incredibly itchy and can get acutely red and sore when I am stressed. At one point when I had dengue fever, I got psoriasis on the palms of my hands.

Lower back pain used to happen to me occasionally but it has recently become what I hope is not a permanent fixture. It requires regular painkillers and visits to the osteopath. It appears that I have one leg slightly shorter than the other so I now have a lift in one shoe. I also receive pain in my hips and hands so I am waiting to see the Rheumatologist.

Migraines occurred after my head injury and I pretty much always had a headache at some level, although it has recently eased off somewhat. Some of these things seemed to be helped by acupuncture and homoeopathy, but not always. Restless leg syndrome affects me often when I am over-tired. It is exhausting trying to sleep when your legs keep moving.

I also got trigeminal neuralgia back in my left ear again in the last year or so. It can most often occur when I am sleeping. This wakes me up and forces me to get up and then re-adjust my position.

I have also recently developed Irritable Bowel Syndrome (IBS) with chronic diarrhoea which makes it difficult when travelling and accentuates the fatigue.

I frequently have hay fever and other allergies that cause my skin to have histamine welts. I don't like to take anti-histamine but I do sometimes.

I recently found out that the kidney stones I had experienced on three occasions were likely a result of sarcoidosis. Unfortunately the last time I had them it was stuck in my ureter and caused hydronephrosis when the kidney swells up and can become damaged. So I now have chronic kidney disease. Since then I have had chronic frequency (needing to urinate) and I am prone to urinary infections. It recently looked like I might have cancer in the bladder but that has been ruled out so I am waiting for further urodynamic studies.

I am very grateful for the National Health Service even though this means appointments can take some time.

Fortunately, I haven't had all of these symptoms at the same time but enough to make it impossible for me in the last few years to hold down a full-time job. It led to me feeling frustrated that with all my experience and training I could not do what I considered was a 'proper job'. But this understanding is changing. I still work hard.

I do believe that "the body keeps the score" and these multiple conditions are a result of the depression and anxiety of my own experiences as well as the vicarious trauma of listening to other's stories.

I admit that I find it disconcerting when people ask you if you are "better now?" It's a really difficult question when you have a chronic illness. The answer is probably "no" or "not at the moment" but I am likely to say "yes", so as not to embarrass them.

Reflection:

More recently, I have realised that the flexibility and grace I have to do what I consider to be important enables me to have a much wider reach. I continue to learn how to rest and achieve a reasonable work-life balance.

Resource:

- *Sarcoidosis UK:* sarcoidosisuk.org

Chapter 70

Surviving Being Struck by Lightning

"Lightning never strikes the same place twice."
British Proverb

I seem to have experienced quite a few challenges when travelling including forgetting passport(s), getting the wrong tickets, planes stuck on the ground and not being allowed off, ridiculously long delays, arriving on the wrong day, etc. It has certainly taken away some of the fun and excitement of travel!

My colleague and friend, Helen, decided that it would not be sensible to travel with me if she was to avoid some of the difficulties. However, we were going to the same conference in Nebraska and as I was getting comfortable in my seat, I saw her walking up the aisle towards me. When she saw me she was close to turning around to go back the way she came but she didn't really have a choice so continued on until she got her seat towards the back of the plane. The plane took off and got to cruising altitude.

As we sat, suddenly there was a jolt and we realised the plane had been struck by lightning and a few minutes later the same thing happened with a second strike. It was alarming to say the least.

We were waiting for an explanation on the tannoy from the pilot but nothing happened. He appeared to be too busy! However, after we arrived and left the plane, the pilot was waiting at the bottom of the stairs to shake our hands and presumably wait for us to say how much we appreciated not being dead.

As I entered the baggage hall, I saw Helen and she rolled her eyes and gave me a look as if to say, 'What the heck! I should have got off when I had the chance!'. However we recently did travel together and nothing happened so I think I am forgiven and we are safe to travel together again.

In fact, when I was working as a camp counsellor in Pennsylvania, USA, I was sitting in the dining hall when there was a storm and just outside the window there was an almighty crash and a tree split down the middle. It had also been a lightning strike.

I had a dear friend called Judith Ennew who was a child rights Professor at Cambridge and she herself was struck by lightning more than once. I wrote about it in a chapter of a book dedicated to her life after she died.

Reflection:

Lightening apparently does strike in the same place more than once. The implication behind the proverb is that you are not likely to experience difficult things multiple times. Hmm. Not sure that is true in my case!

Resource:

- 10 Striking facts about lightning: <u>metoffice.gov-.uk/weather/learn-about/weather/types-of-weather/thunder-and-lightning/facts-about-lightning</u>

Chapter 71

Surviving an Earthquake

"There is a lot that happens around the world we cannot control. We cannot stop earthquakes, ...but when we know where the hungry, the homeless and the sick exist, then we can help."

Jan Schakowsky

Over the years I have gone to a range of conferences and consultations all over the world, mostly on child safeguarding and human trafficking. In the beginning I was going primarily to learn, but later I was usually presenting. I have been to Australia, Bosnia-Helgavosia, Cambodia, Canada, Ecuador, England, Hong Kong, Italy, Japan, Malaysia, the Netherlands, Northern Ireland, Poland, Portugal, Qatar, Scotland, Thailand, Wales and the US of A.

The great thing about going to conferences is the networking you can do and being able to see and experience another culture. Of course, you also need to get there and travelling is not as much fun as it used to be for me, but I love it when I get there and enjoy meeting interesting people.

However there is a downside. Travelling away from the family was not always good. Siobhan often had to deal with things on her own without my support. For example, one time when I was in Poland she told me that she had developed a nasty fungal infection in her foot that was tracking up her leg which required IV antibiotics. She needed me home but it was too far. Another time she had just been badly injured when the generator winder became dislodged and hit her in the face, but I left her when she really needed my support. Things seemed to happen more often when I was away.

Another disadvantage of conferences was unless you were in the in-crowd then you were not invited to speak in the plenary sessions, which are the sessions everyone goes to hear. Most of the time I was speaking on topics that were only of interest to a minority of people. It may have been a topic that I thought was important for everyone to hear, such as the sexual exploitation of boys and young men, but it wasn't enough for those organising the conference to think that. I remember one session where there were only four people who turned up. All the work in preparation and flying around the planet for only four people was not good. I tried to convince myself that if only one person found it helpful then it was worth it but I'm not sure that was really true.

Topics I have talked about are very varied but the key ones are; a) Sexual exploitation of boys and young men b) Sexual exploitation of transgender c) Learning from doing advocacy d) Addressing demand of sexual violence e) Learnings from the Butterfly project f) How is research important for anti-trafficking efforts. This year (2024) I am speaking on g) Lessons learnt from 12 years of researching sexual exploitation of men and boys and h) Faith Based Organisations unhelpful portrayal of Survivors of Trafficking.

If I was to do conferences again I would be much more selective. One of my friends said, "If they don't pay for you to go then don't go". If I had done that I might not have gone anywhere but certainly as I get older it is not as possible as it was before. Fortunately, many conferences are now done wholly, or partly, online (hybrid) and over COVID I spoke in about ten locations around the world from the comfort of my own home.

One international conference I have attended regularly in the States has really evolved over the years. Initially it was mostly American women but over the years it has become more international. It started with outreach focusing only on the sexual exploitation of women and girls but over the years has expanded to boys, men and transgender. It started by focusing on survivors but then later understood the importance of addressing demand - including pornography and sex buyers. I believe I had some influence on some of that.

At one conference I went to in Australia I was going to include in my talk about *Nestlé* being unethical in the way they promote bottle feeding over breastfeeding. When I arrived at the conference I found out that they were one of the co-sponsors! One of the organisers asked me to take that part out of my talk. I asked if I could talk to a representative of the Sydney office of *Nestlé* and explain what I was about to do. Of course he was shocked that his company could do anything unethical but I provided some evidence I had with me. I included it in my talk.

One conference I went to in Thailand we were in between sessions and there was an earthquake. I don't know whether it was because I had a bit of PTSD going on but I really thought that the massive hotel we were in was going to collapse any minute. Most people seemed completely oblivious to what had just happened but I remembered Siobhan talking about the San Francisco earthquake that she witnessed and with my previous traumatic experiences it took me a few minutes to realise and believe we were going to be OK.

Reflection:

In retrospect I should have been more selective about attending some of the conferences and used the money more usefully. But I believe it is important to learn and teach.

Resources:

- Why Asia Pacific is so prone to natural disasters: <u>weforum.org/agenda/2018/12/why-asia-pacific-is-especially-prone-to-natural-disasters</u>
- Staying safe in an earthquake: <u>redcross.org/get-help/how-to-prepare-for-emergencies/types-of-emergencies/earthquake.html</u>

Chapter 72

Surviving Academia

"When husked rice stands up it becomes unproductive, when bent down it becomes productive"
(*Humbleness earns other people's respect and appreciation*)
Cambodian Proverb

After graduating with my PhD I tried working for short periods at both of the Universities in Swansea as a lecturer in child public health, a lecturer in child safeguarding, and a researcher with Roma, Gypsy, and Travellers. The latter job was for a year but I had to take three months off because I became unwell. My manager unfairly told me that I would not be named on the final published papers even though I had done a lot of the work. Not getting published is equivalent in academia to not working.

I had to fight for my right to be included even though it was clear in the university's policy that I should. This confirmed to me that I much preferred working with NGOs to Universities where I was more established. But it meant that I would have no stable income from the work I did.

In Southeast Asia, Jarrett and I published most of our research in reports (English and a summary in the main local languages) so that it could be used locally. Later we decided to get our research published in peer-reviewed journals so that the international NGO and academic community were able to benefit from our findings.

We made a special effort to get our work mainly published in journals that were free to both authors and also to readers where possible to avoid people in the majority South (developing world) having to go through a paywall to access papers. This wasn't that easy. Some publishers can charge up to 4,000 USD for papers to be open access!

In 2021, I managed to persuade the peer-reviewed and open-access journal *Dignity* to do a special edition on the *Butterfly Longitudinal Research Project*. It took me and James over a year to pull it all together but it was satisfying to see it finally published and it is now freely accessible to anyone who wants to read it in English for free.

In 2022 I was awarded one of the 3 'Most Influential Scholars' from the *Global Association of Human Trafficking Scholars/University of Toledo*. Jarrett and later Professor Madeleine (we three are known as the Mad Jargle) also received one! We are now on the Executive Committee making suggestions to create more access for people from the Global South (developing world).

I am currently (2024) working with the *Journal of Human Trafficking* on a series of research articles on Survivors Voices including voices from Asia, Europe, Africa and the States.

Jarrett, Madeleine and I are currently exploring how we can support people who want to do research without relying on the very narrow approach to research that most Universities allow.

Reflection:

Academia, like all fields of work, can be a challenging place to work. Working for charities/non-government organisations can be surprisingly challenging too. I sometimes think that the lack of money means some people seek other more negative ways to accrue power.

Resource:

- *Global Association of Human Trafficking Scholars* (which is an excellent resource network): gahts.com

Or scan me instead!

Chapter 73

Surviving the Loss of my Soul Mate and Best Friend

"Everything you have in this world is borrowed for a short time."
Welsh Proverb

A year after we arrived back in the UK we went on a family holiday to Scotland and stayed in the house of a friend. As the week went on Siobhan wasn't feeling very well so she stayed in bed. Occasionally she had a migraine and retreated to bed and I thought it was something like that. The day before we were due to go home she was feeling worse so we decided to go to the airport in a taxi rather than the rented car we had. We were glad to be flying back to Cardiff rather than driving back to Wales. Zoe and Hannah had already left by train and Sarah was with us.

We also got a taxi back home from the airport. I asked Siobhan if she wanted to stop at the hospital but she said she didn't. We arrived home and I called the doctor in the hope they might come out. They told me to keep her hydrated and bring her to the GP surgery in the morning. By around 6pm she seemed to be a little worse so I called the doctor again. They repeated what the previous doctor had said.

Then at around 9.30pm whilst I was downstairs making a mug of tea I heard Siobhan call out. I went upstairs and realised that she couldn't move her arms and legs. I thought she had a stroke but that is usually one-sided. I called 999 emergency services and asked for an ambulance. They talked me through what to do and confirmed it wasn't a stroke.

The ambulance arrived after around 30 minutes and the paramedics put up a drip and took some blood. They helped her to get in the ambulance. As I don't drive I asked if Sarah and I could also come in the ambulance and they agreed.

We were 'blue-lighted' down the hill from our house and just as we were turning the corner Siobhan's heart stopped and they had to resuscitate her in front of us. We got to the hospital very quickly and she was taken into the Resuscitation room where the serious emergencies go.

Sarah and I held each other's hands and waited. After what seemed like hours someone came out and said that she was not doing well. I understood then that this meant she would be in ITU for a few days.

We didn't hear until later that they were trying to resuscitate her many times and it wasn't working. Sarah and I still agree that we heard Siobhan call out and believe that it was her saying goodbye to us.

Finally, the consultant doctor and head nurse came out

and told us that she had died. We were both shocked. We couldn't quite take it in. But they brought her body out to a side room and we could go and be with the body. If you have ever seen a dead body you know that the spirit is no longer there. However, her face was still a little bit warm so I kissed her goodbye.

I called my pastor Chris, and his wife Barbara, and they turned up as soon as they could. The police came in and gave us her rings. I didn't know what to do. After all the forms were completed we went home. Chris and Barbara took us to the house. It was around 6am. I went into the house and walked up the stairs to bed. Plastic bags and tubes were left over on the bed and floor from the para-medic and Siobhan's nursing uniform was on the back of the wardrobe door. It was awful.

Later my pastor Chris took me out for tea and we talked about Siobhan. I received a card from someone and on the envelope it read Glenn rather than Glenn & Siobhan. I would never receive a card for both of us ever again.

It wasn't until we got the report from the coroner about 6 months later that we heard she had died of sepsis, secondary to a kidney infection (pyelonephritis), a painful and unpleasant illness caused by bacteria travelling from your bladder into one or both of your kidneys. Sepsis is actually the most common preventable illness but only if you catch it quickly.

I do love **all** my daughters/offspring. They are all gifted in different ways and are all gorgeous. But after Siobhan died it was tough. We were all grieving and hurting and trying to come to terms with being without her. It was only a year after we had left Cambodia when she died so I wanted us to go back there and have a memorial service there. I also wanted us to go to California to enable Siobhan's family and friends to grieve at a memorial service.

We had asked the funeral director to put the ashes in 3 metal flasks so that we could spread her ashes in 3 locations. The first we did with my brother Nick and sister-in-law Fiona on the beautiful cliffs in Gower close to where we live in Wales. We had a service at Linden church and it was lovely being with so many dear friends from over the years.

The second was in Cambodia, Kampot, on the river at night amongst fire-flies in trees, and with dear Carrie's help, we sprinkled them off the side of a boat. We also had a church service in Phnom Penh.

The third service was in Berkeley where we had got married and we sprinkled ashes in Halfmoon Bay close to my mother-in-law and Siobhan's family in the Bay area, California.

About a year after Siobhan died I was invited to tell my story in an audio presentation with slides as a way which enabled patients, and patient's relatives, to explain what had happened to them so that the hospital could improve their policy and programmes. This was part of a new storytelling program. I used the opportunity to express concern over the way in which we as a family were not informed quickly enough about what was going on. Unfortunately, the accident and emergency department got a bit fixated on the time I said it took which they said was shorter. However, I was able to use the story with the Sepsis Society and also as a guest lecturer in a course for End of Life practitioners.

I asked if they would consider changing the resuscitation policy to one in which families could receive support by a dedicated nurse. I later had the opportunity to speak to the hospital resuscitation board and was reassured that things would improve. But I am not sure if they really did do anything.

A much better understanding of Sepsis has happened since Siobhan died. It is recognised in the UK as the leading cause of preventable death. Dedicated sepsis staff are now in most hospitals.

Reflection:

Whichever way someone dies it is still a terrible shock. We had no idea she was going to go so quickly. Just a few hours before we thought she had had a flu virus or something simple.

Resources:

- Dealing with sudden unexpected death: sudden.org/about-sudden-death

Or scan me instead!

- *The Sepsis Manual*: sepsistrust.org/wp-content/uploads/2022/06/Sepsis-Manual-Sixth-Edition.pdf

Chapter 74

Surviving Being a Single Dad of a Single Mum

"Going into a pregnancy is a really challenging time for a woman, because it's forever-changing, both mentally and physically."
Brooke Burke

L ess than a year after Siobhan died Sarah said she needed to talk to me. I knew straight away what that meant. She emptied a carrier bag with about ten pregnancy tests, all reading positive! She was definitely pregnant. I slowly asked her what she wanted to do about it and promised I would support her whatever she decided. She decided to go ahead with the pregnancy which was very brave of her. It also sadly meant that she was not able to complete her A levels.

During Sarah's pregnancy, the person I most wanted to receive input from, Siobhan, wasn't there. But it was surprisingly helpful to imagine what she would have said.

The pregnancy went well but Sarah was very anaemic and the normal iron pills and medicine were insufficient, so she needed to have an iron intravenous infusion. I offered to come with her to the hospital but she said it was fine and unnecessary. As she was sitting in the chair hooked up to the drip she suddenly felt awful. Unknown to her she was going into anaphylactic shock. When someone realised what was happening the red button on the wall was pushed and suddenly she was surrounded by doctors and nurses doing their thing to resuscitate her. I felt awful that I hadn't been able to be with her. As is her normal, Sarah recovered amazingly well from the ordeal and the pregnancy continued.

Sarah woke up one morning and said she had a back-ache. I asked her if she thought she was going into labour. She said she didn't know because she had never been in labour before. Of course, I wasn't much help because neither had I! I suggested she call the midwife which she did. The midwife said not to worry, to take her time and that she would be along shortly. It was the first pregnancy after all. But by the time the midwife arrived, she was getting quite uncomfortable.

When the midwife arrived and checked her she was already 6cm and this quickly increased to 8cm. We called our neighbour, Sarah's chosen driver, who was also her assigned advocate, and drove her to the hospital. Sarah was apparently not wanting to stay put so a number of people were called in to ensure she stayed in bed. It all happened pretty quickly.

Sarah's boyfriend's mum turned up and she texted whilst she was in the delivery suite to say Sarah was doing well. I was disappointed I couldn't be with Sarah but at least she was able to support her son.

Within a relatively short time, her sisters and I were in the waiting room and the midwife informed us that we were aunties and a grandad. What a wonderful experience it was to finally be with her and to welcome Teddy, the most beautiful baby in the world.

Reflection:

When Sarah first told me it seemed like another disastrous challenge for all of us but now my grandson Teddy is in the world we couldn't love him more.

Resources:

- Information for Single Dads:
  gingerbread.org.uk/find-information/parenting-perspectives/single-dads
- Information for Single Mums:
  familylives.org.uk/advice/your-family/single-parents/advice-on-becoming-a-single-parent

Chapter 75

Surviving Fatherhood

"Whatever you are, be a good one."
Cambodian Proverb

Being a dad is one of the best things that ever happened to me. I have a T-shirt for Halloween that says "You can't scare me. I have 3 Daughters".

Seeing Zoe when they were born with their bright orange hair took my breath away and they continue to take my breath away with their determination, intelligence, thoughtful passion for justice and wit. I am deeply proud of who they were and who they are becoming. Zoe works for a women's cooperative in an inner city part of London and lives on a beautiful old Dutch tulip barge with her partner, Will. Will had their own survival but that is their story. The initial fear of losing Zoe and their mother in the emergency caesarian section was terrifying.

In contrast Hannah was always the sensitive, kind, zany, joker who everyone adores and whom she makes them feel loved. It is impossible to get a good photo of her because she always pulls a face. She is an extraordinary fine artist and has created wall murals in restaurants and hotels. She is a carer and works with a family with an autistic daughter who she keeps safe. She also lives in a narrow barge boat.

Sarah and I have always had a bit of a tumultuous relationship but we are reminding each other, now more than ever, how much we love each other. It took Sarah a while to trust me having been brought up in an orphanage of primarily women carers but once we bonded, it stuck. But it wasn't always easy.

When we first came to the UK I was initially without Siobhan and the immigration officer said we had the wrong visa. It took some explaining to say we were just visiting and would provide the adoption papers on our next visit. So fortunately rather than being arrested for child trafficking we were given the appropriate stamp and walked on!

When we lived in Swansea when the children were still small we did the MacMillan Cancer Charity sponsored 22-mile walk three times. It was quite an achievement, especially for Sarah who was about 6 years old at the time! We did ask them to take her pushchair to the next station several times in case we needed it, but we didn't, and when we arrived she wanted to go to the park! It showed once again how resilient she is. We had no idea supporting this charity would soon have a personal connection.

One time when living in Wales I was taking Sarah to primary school in Wales. She was being her defiant self and didn't want to go to school. We had to walk as I didn't drive. So at one point I was, what must have appeared to be, dragging her down the street, shouting at her to walk on her own. A woman in a people carrier van stopped on the curb and called out to me "I am watching you!". I was already upset and this really didn't help. She continued to follow me slowly and we finally got to school. I had visions of being reported to the police and getting into the local paper!

When I asked the children about their most happy memories Hannah said she remembered walking down the stairs of our wooden house and asked if we could have ice cream for breakfast, and I said I was thinking the same thing. Sarah said she loved how I would pick her up from school on a Friday afternoon and we would head for the Swimming Pool next to the school. Zoe said she remembered the infamous Easter Egg treasure hunt for our expat community's children with various clues hidden around the house finally ending in the fridge where the Easter Egg waited to be found. Isn't it interesting they chose such simple family things, rather than our travel to exotic locations?

One time we were walking through customs in Cambodia and the officials saw something in the scanner machine. We were pulled to one side and presented with scissors which Sarah had decided she needed to "make stuff" on the flight. They were quickly confiscated.

Another time we were visiting a temple in Bali and a monkey walked straight up to us, walked up Sarah's torso and stole her water bottle from right under our noses. It was clear who was in charge of this area!

One time when I left Cambodia I asked my colleague Romanea what he had learned most from the 5 years we had worked together. Rather than all the work we had done, he said he learnt about fatherhood from me which was very touching. I think that many people lacked good role models after the genocide. Family violence was too normal. I was by no means a perfect father but most of the time I tried to love my children with dignity and love.

Zoe and Hannah continue to live in London on separate canal boats. I measure the amount of time there on how many winters they survive! So far it is quite a few. Zoe and Matt also live on an old Dutch Tulip barge, which is beautiful. Hannah has just brought her own barge too.

Reflection:

It has been a tumultuous time since Siobhan died. The girls were angry with me and angry with life. But we all stuck in there and now we are good. I love each of them so much it hurts. And they tell me they love me too.

Resource:

- Parenting life of the father of four daughters: <u>boredpanda.com/parenting-life-father-of-daughter-simon-hooper</u>

Chapter 76

Surviving Grandfatherhood.

"Love your children one tao (unit of measurement, a large basket to put rice in). Love your grandchildren one thiang (one thiang is equivalent to 2 taos)."
Cambodian Proverb

When we lived in Cambodia we visited a family shortly after we had been robbed when we were looking for a new place to live. The house was newly built and they obviously had a big family with many children running around. Siobhan, being her usual friendly self, got into conversation with the matriarch living in the house. She was trying to explain how she didn't like robbers after our burglary but the word for robber in Khmer language is very close to grandchildren so she was effectively saying she didn't like grandchildren! Needless to say, they didn't offer us to come back for a second viewing!

Being a grandad has been a wonderful privilege and also very hard. It was complicated. Sarah and Teddy lived with me for the first few years. I adored having Teddy around. People would say the best thing about being a grandad is that you can give them back at the end of the day. Well, it wasn't quite like that because we lived in the same house! As someone who had experience caring for Zoe as a baby, apart from my Child Health nursing experience, it wasn't something I was worried about. But I wasn't as young as I was before! Sarah needed to go to work and she got work at a cafe on the pier. It was hard work for me to care for Teddy and push him around in his buggy/pushchair.

Sarah struggled with not having her mother and, in addition, her boyfriend whom she had the baby with left her shortly after she had delivered. His family wanted access to Teddy and put pressure on Sarah. We were fine with his dad visiting our house whilst she was breastfeeding but they wanted to take him away. They later took Sarah to court for access and over time their access to Teddy increased to half time. In some ways, I was glad that this happened because I feel that often in a separation of a couple the father does not have the opportunity to have the access he really should have.

As Teddy got older he went to pre-Kindergarten and I would take him and collect him. The school was a few miles away, closer to Teddy's dad, so I would get a bus (sometimes two) on the way and walk him home. We would often stop by the park and meet my friend Barbara. So about half the time Teddy was with us I would be with him all day until just before bed-time. It was exhausting but I loved/love being with him.

There is a story here I would like to have included but it is a story that is primarily someone else's and they asked that it should be excluded.

What I can say is that Sarah is one of the most resilient

323

people on the planet. She lost her biological mum and then her adoptive mum and then her boyfriend and her baby for a lot of the time. She has had several operations on her cleft palate and it still isn't finished. I feel that she has been let down by the health social services and court systems. But in spite of everything she remains a loving mother, sister and daughter. She has continued to work hard in cafes and restaurants in spite of racism. I am proud of her.

Reflection:

Grandparenthood is a truly wonderful experience

Resource:

- Advice for grandparents:
  ageuk.org.uk/information-advice/health-wellbeing/relationships-family/top-tips-for-grandparents

Chapter 77

Surviving People's Wrong Assumptions and Prejudices (including my own)

"Stop judging by mere appearances, but instead judge correctly."*
John 7: 24

"Prejudice is a great time saver. You can form opinions without having to get the facts."
E. B. White

People can quickly make assumptions about Sarah and me being in public together without checking them. There are several occasions when this was incredibly awkward, not to say painful. Scripture tells us on many occasions not to make assumptions about people as above.

The first was when we were in Cambodia and unbeknown to us a video was taken of us sitting on a park bench together. That video was then used in a promotion video on social media for a medium-sized NGO/charity. A section of the video showed our backs sitting together, the voice in the video's background talking about paedophiles coming to Cambodia!

Fortunately, several friends saw the video and informed me as soon as they saw it so that I was able to meet with the CEO to ask him to take it down ASAP. The thing that frustrated me was that they took the video, but did not approach me or contact someone and report me. If that had happened it could have been quickly resolved and I would have congratulated them! Instead I was left to contact the Director myself and ask him to take the video down. He knew me so it was quickly achieved.

Another time was when I was on the bus in Swansea with Sarah and Teddy and as we headed to the back of the bus people looked aghast at us, or smirked at us. It was clear that they considered that I must have obtained Sarah as a child bride. I told Sarah to call me her dad more loudly than normal but it was another frustrating example of people making wrong assumptions which was ironic when my job has primarily been involved in addressing sex trafficking. I have subsequently bought another T-shirt. On the front it says, "She is my daughter..." and on the back, "But thank you for your concern! Call *'Stop the Traffick'*!"

When Sarah was six months pregnant I went with her for her scan. Shortly after we arrived she was whisked away into a side room and asked if she was safe. They were concerned that I might be trafficking her. She assured them I was her dad and they then continued with the scan.

At a later time, someone accused me of making connections with a young relative on social media. It was something I would never do and I still don't know how it happened but rightly the accusation was taken seriously and I had to go through a safeguarding process. It was disturbing to be on the other side of the fence again; accused of being a perpetrator. Later, I sought and was forgiven for what had happened and it was good to be reconciled again.

I know that I am not innocent of making wrong assumptions. I consider myself to have good emotional intelligence but I do tend to err on the positive rather than the negative and this can go against me. Hiring an intern who turned out to be mentally ill was a big mistake and we had to deal with the fallout of that.

But the situation that took some time to recover from was finding out that someone who lived close to us was actually a paedophile. He himself had children, and were Christians, so we had a lot in common. He and his wife were extremely affable and their household was always open to borrowing sugar or pop in for a cup of tea. They had plans to head to the mission field and when they did we inherited their cat. We also provided some financial support to them.

Several years later they returned to the UK and I bumped into them a couple of times. To me, I always felt good after I had talked to him. But it was a while later when I found out that he was in prison. It seemed incredulous but he had been entrapped by a special branch of police who had been speaking to him as a 12-year-old girl. He had invited 'her' to have sex with him. He was arrested and is still in jail. I felt so sad for his wife and family and for the way his life has in many ways effectively ended.

On one flight to the UK they did a more intense check than usual and pulled me over to the side. I had previously put on some ointment for my psoriasis that left a residue on my hands. The residue, for some reason, made the alarm go off so I had to be taken to a side room for a 'full' examination. I took my clothes off and they did the required examination with a 'wand'. Fortunately, they did not do a rectal examination as I was expecting and I was relieved when they said I could go! It was another example of being misconstrued.

Another time I was in the secondary immigration waiting area in the States and a guy there was having a very hard time. He told me that he was coming to the States to receive an award for his life of humanitarian service but the department didn't care about that. The poor guy was humiliated and made to feel like a criminal. He just wanted to go home.

Reflection:

I think it is better to think the best of someone and then find out later that you were wrong than to think the worst of someone and then find out later that they were good people. But we all need to learn to not make assumptions based on looks.

Resource:

- The sin of making assumptions: thescribesportion.com/sin-making-assumptions

Chapter 78

Surviving Being an Abused Landlord

"We are only tenants, and shortly the great Landlord will give us notice that our lease has expired."
Joseph Jefferso

In the black-and-white movies, the landlord is portrayed as a wicked man who forces his tenants to pay exorbitant rents and then evicts them at a moment's notice! In my case the reverse happened. The tenant exploited me!

I was able to buy a small house in addition to the one we already had which was perfect for Sarah and Teddy to move into. I had got it from savings and the mortgage death insurance. The house was a two bedroomed house and I fitted it out so it was very nice and comfortable. Some friends from Cambodia stayed there while they were at a local Bible college and they looked after it well.

But shortly after moving in they told me that water was pouring down one of the walls in all four rooms connected to the external wall! It was the end of the terrace. Even though I had a surveyor, they had not picked up on this. The builders did a good job fixing it but I had a huge bill which was equivalent to two years rent! I was so frustrated.

After the friends from Cambodia left, I heard about a refugee who had been working part-time for the church and needed accommodation so I offered it to him for a more than reasonable amount, and he moved in. We initially got on well and I was pleased to be able to help him out by keeping the rent down and doing everything he requested. However, it became apparent when we needed him to leave so that Sarah could move in, that he wasn't going to leave without a lot of hassle.

At first, we gave him informal notice but at the end of the day he wasn't going anywhere, so we had to start again using formal processes. Then we did it 'by the book' and he still didn't leave. So then we went to court which in itself was a lengthy and expensive process. It wasn't until he was under the threat of bailiffs that he left and when he left he took much of my stuff with him!

He took so much of my stuff but the solicitor told me unless it was worth a huge amount it wasn't worth trying to get any money out of him. I just had to let it go. I had initially provided him with a nice home beautifully equipped with everything down to sheets and towels and his thank you was to exploit me.

So it took more than two years for us to get the house back. I had it fixed up again and got new furniture and house supplies and Sarah was able to move in.

Reflection:

There is a myth that if you are abused then you will become an abuser but of course there is an alternative. You can choose to be kind instead.

Resource:

- *National Residential Landlords Association:* nrla.org.uk

Chapter 79

Surviving Grief

"Love is composed of a single soul inhabiting two bodies."
Aristotle

Losing Siobhan was a terrible loss. We had been through so much together. Even after nearly eight years apart I still think of her and miss her most days. Sometimes I imagine what it would be like if we were still together. For example, I dreamed of what might it have been like if we both woke up to our grandson Teddy coming into our bedroom and telling us that the Easter bunny had arrived! I realise just how hard it is for others who are grieving and how much we have lost in the Minority North (West) from not having a more extended time to grieve.

Just before she got pregnant Sarah begged me to get a dog. Initially I was reluctant to take on the responsibility but finally gave in. We got a cockapoo and like many others will vouch, Wallace (or Wally for short) became our comfort and joy. Apart from the normal, to be expected, puppy accidents she was so great to have around when we were feeling low. When you looked into those beautiful brown eyes you just sensed that she knew you needed some puppy love, and she knew how to make you feel loved.

I was incredibly grateful to be part of a loving community church called Linden. They welcomed us when we first arrived in Swansea from Cambodia, they supported us when Siobhan got cancer, they celebrated with us when Sarah's final Welsh adoption came through and when I passed my PhD. They grieved with us when Siobhan died and they have supported me in the grief process.

I have also maintained friendships from my time working overseas. The bond we share from being together in challenging situations around the world is indisputable. Many have gone on to do amazing things, often working in health, social and justice fields.

I wanted a special event for my 60th birthday. My dear friend Carrie who had helped to organise the special event to spread ashes on the boat in Kampot, Cambodia, also helped me to have a special ceremony on the Gower coastline. It was by Siobhan's bench, which we festooned with flowers, and then my friends and I walked up to the local castle. It was an important time for me to move on from the wonderful relationship I had with Siobhan to be open to a new life without her. The small group of friends held a ball of wool and threw it to each other with me in the middle to symbolise my network of friendships. I was then presented with a beautiful ring which I wear every day. It is silver with a Celtic symbol in the middle made in Welsh gold. A very precious reminder to me that I am loved by God and my friends.

Just before the COVID pandemic I attended a two-week Death Doula course. A doula is usually someone who supports the mother through the birth process. A death doula is someone who helps the dying person through the death process. There were about 25 people from different faith backgrounds and I was really impressed by the deep sense of kindness and peace of everyone there. The purpose was to learn how to be with people in their final days and hours and support the families afterwards. Beautiful people and many lessons learnt.

After my youngest daughter Sarah moved out of the house it was the first time I was left on my own, but not for long. I decided that I really wanted to help a refugee family fleeing from Ukraine. So I completed the forms and within a short time, I had connected to a single mum and her two children. I had thought we could all live in the same house but that became impossible when I realised the children were a 17-year-old boy and a 12-year-old girl.

They had approval quicker than I expected and it happened on one of my trips overseas. My friend Barbara not only offered me a room in her house but also helped them on their arrival to get them settled into my house while I was on one of my trips. Within a short time, I was able to find, with the help of friends, jobs for both the mother Viktoria and the oldest son, Haman.

I am still living in my housemate Barbara's house with no indication that either the war will end or that they will find an alternative place to live, but I am enjoying living there. Wally, my dog, has made tentative friends with Barbara's cat Reggie and we currently all live together as a happy family. My daughter Sarah gave us a joking sign for Christmas that read, "A lovely lady and a grumpy old git live here'.

Reflection:

Some days I still wake up and think how much I miss Siobhan. She is often in my mind. I am grateful for the love we shared.

Resource:

- *Death Doula* training: eol-doula.uk/our-training

Chapter 80

Surviving Toxic Masculinity

"Plates in a basket will rattle."
Cambodian Proverb

This is a sad proverb because it implies that domestic violence is inevitable, usually meaning men against women or children.

People often assume that toxic masculinity only affects women, but they are wrong. Toxic masculinity has affected me as a child and as an adult. Bullies have told me as a boy and man to "man up". It has affected me in society's ongoing patriarchy which says I should take my responsibility as a man. Being a 'real man' according to them means playing men's games such as rugby and football, drinking lots of beer, and having sex with lots of women. You know the drill. But what about those of us who don't fit the stereotype?

I find that even admitting to being chronically ill is seen as effeminate. So as men we shut up, we don't go to the doctor until it's too late and we struggle with pain. Recent joking about 'man flu' implies that men are generally hypochondriacs who can't cope with being ill.

I was recently on a train and I was wearing a rugby shirt given to me by a friend. I got talking with someone and they asked me if I played. Well of course I didn't, and hadn't, but I had this strong urge to lie to make me appear more masculine so I said I had done in the past. He asked me what position I played and then I was stuck! I knew so little about rugby that I couldn't answer so I mumbled something about defence. I got more and more embarrassed so I had to back off and sit somewhere else. Ridiculous I know. What was I thinking and why did I feel the need to do it?

Shortly after Siobhan and I were married we were walking in Berkeley, California, when a guy walked past with a pair of trainers and a backpack and nothing else. We later found out he was the 'naked guy', the student who preferred not to wear clothes. The University had to create a new policy that students should wear clothes in class!

A few years ago when I was spending a couple of months in Cambodia I got some tattoos done on both arms. The tattoo artist said that if I came back he could do the tattoos in the bar, then he would give them to me for half price. So of the three sessions I got two for half price. It was surprisingly not as painful as I expected although the colours were more painful than the outlines. I asked him to tattoo pictures of butterflies. Each one represented a family member. All of them are beautiful but my favourite and the one people like most is Siobhan's butterfly, a beautiful aqua blue colour butterfly from California and her favourite colour. It is amusing that tattoos were always a very masculine thing but nowadays everyone seems to enjoy them.

I was recently walking along the promenade by the

beach in my hometown and got talking to an older man probably aged in his eighties. I was dressed in a sweater and thick coat but he had a light sweater only. I asked him if he was cold. He said he didn't need a coat; he was a **real** man. So apparently real men don't need to wear coats!

In contrast to this toxic masculinity, I really enjoyed attending the *Male Rites of Passage* in Ireland. It was a wonderful way to experience masculine spirituality full of symbols and rites helping men to consider what is important in their lives. I would recommend this to every man to attend and reflect on what masculinity really is and what it is not. It was a very powerful experience. I have also enjoyed listening to the *Stories of Men* podcast.

I have enjoyed getting to know some of the men in the *Christian Vision for Men* Wales group. They didn't seem to know what to do with a gay Christian man when I first came out but they seem to have accepted me now.

Reflection:

As men we need to consider what it means to be a man, and what it doesn't.

Resources:

- Male rites of passage: <u>malejourney.org.uk/rites</u>

Or scan me instead!

- *Stories of Men* podcast: <u>podcasts.apple.com/us/ podcast/stories-of-men-beneath-the-surface/ id1546893090?ign-itscg=30200&ign-itsct= podcast_box</u>
- *Christian Vision for Men (CVM):* <u>cvm.org.uk</u>

Chapter 81

Surviving the Disturbing Impact of the P*rnography Industry

"Stolen water is sweet, food eaten in secret is delicious."
Proverbs 9:17

P*rnography is an insidious part of our culture and increasingly many other cultures worldwide. The p*rn industry is making billions of dollars. We are exposed to it every day and children are exposed to it younger and younger. I believe there is a strong link between p*rn and trafficking and I have written about it in 'Finding our Way Through the Traffick: Navigating our way through the complexities of a Christian response to sexual exploitation and Human Trafficking' (Regnum 2017).

Early research we conducted in Cambodia on access to p*rn was when you could buy CDs for 1 USD. We found that children were rummaging through very explicit p*rn involving children and even animals. Although shops selling DVDs initially had this material on shelves in the front they were soon hidden around the back, but if children saw them nobody stopped them.

One time when I was doing some work in the provinces I stayed in a local hotel. In the evening they would play p*rn on all the TVs, including p*rn involving children for the guests to see. It was sickening and showed how normalised it was becoming.

I decided to conduct research on whether Christian missionaries and development workers accessed porn and prostitutes. I didn't want to be seen as looking at tourists if we weren't looking at ourselves. Surprisingly to some, especially women, around 10% of men did buy sex. We took the results to different international churches and men's groups to encourage NGOs to consider how they could support men who were honest enough to admit they had a problem. A men's accountability group was started in Phnom Penh that has helped many men. This research was later published in the *Evangelical Missionary Quarterly*.

In the UK I conducted a similar research project with Christian men through the evangelical men's organisation *Christian Vision for Men* and with support from *Naked Truth*. Initially they were not sure if they wanted to do it but they did agree and we had over 500 anonymous respondents. It was published in *Dignity Journal*.

I have a great T-shirt that reads 'P*rn Kills Love'. It's a good reminder that p*rn is not about a relationship, but about self-gratification. It is produced by the organisation *Fight the New Drug* which does great advocacy work with the P*rn industry including at p*rn conventions where they give Bibles to p*rn stars saying "Jesus loves P*rn stars!". The power of this statement is that it is the last thing that p*rn stars would expect to hear when it is exactly what they need to hear.

We developed a flipbook for children to make good choices when it comes to p*rn www.asianyouthagainst porn.org but we need parents and teachers to take it seriously and not say "boys will be boys". Incidentally it is becoming an increasing problem for girls.

I subsequently did research in Germany and there is interest in doing similar studies in Portugal and the Czech Republic. These studies are not to point the finger at men and say they're 'naughty boys' but to try to encourage Christian men to talk about the very real challenges they face that I believe are reducing men's self-confidence, breaking up marriages and leading to an epidemic of mental health issues in men. It also impacts human trafficking as people want to try what they see.

I admit that I still struggle with p*rnography and have joined an online group of men who support each other. It's a long journey.

Reflection:

How can we challenge the megalithic p*rn industry? How can we help children to not watch p*rn and see its harms without the huge burden of guilt?

Resources:

- *Naked Truth Project*: <u>nakedtruthproject.com</u>

Or scan me instead!

- Sexual behaviour of Men in the Church in the UK conducted by Tim and I: <u>digitalcommons.uri.edu/dignity/vol8/iss1/7</u>

Or scan me instead!

- CVM Podcasts: <u>codelife.podbean.-com/e/codelife-special-edition-part-1</u>
- <u>codelife.podbean.com/e/codelife-special-edition-part-2</u>

Chapter 82

Surviving Homophobia and Coming Out as a Gay Man

"The world breaks everyone and afterwards, many are strong in the broken places."
Ernest Hemmingway

I remember one time before I was married when a guy friend who I was very fond of came up behind me to hug me when I was sitting down. My heart stopped and melted at the same time. This felt completely natural. He genuinely loved me, never mind if it was sexual or not, and I could completely feel it.

For Siobhan, she really didn't like me talking about my attraction to men at all and this was incredibly hard for me. There were very few people I did tell, but it felt awkward.

At the memorial service in Cambodia, there was a misunderstanding and I had to talk to the girls about my sexuality. They were a little disconcerted that it happened there and then but regarding the issue they were fine. In fact, Zoe, my oldest child, had recently come out as queer and later chose the pronoun they/them and being gender fluid.

After that, I came out to my siblings. I wasn't sure how they would respond but they were all fine about it. I was grateful for this, knowing many whose families were not so accepting.

I then came out to my current church family. The pastor Chris, was thoughtful and kind which I expected having known him for many years. I told him my concern was that people would think my marriage was a sham, but he knew us both well enough to know that there was a deep love that we had for each other and reassured me that no one who really knew us would think that.

After Siobhan died I couldn't immediately even think about going into another relationship with anyone. But I had one dear woman friend and we hung out a lot even though she lived in another country. We were close friends but she asked me where it was going. I realised that it was too hard for her, and for me, to leave it unspoken so I told her that whilst I loved her as a friend, I realised that it wouldn't be fair on either her or me for it to develop into anything more. It was painful to separate but it was the right thing to do.

I realise that for some people there is an "Eww" factor where they can't bear to think about a man putting his penis anywhere near another man. It just makes them feel physically sick. One friend said to me, "It's just so unnatural".

We talked about how other Christian friends, churches, and organisations might respond to me coming out, recognising that for some it would be 'challenging'. I considered whether I could just allow it to happen as and when but I felt that it was too complicated to really do that. *I realised that I had a choice. Either keep lying or tell the truth.* I have a large following on Facebook and I announced it and braced myself for the response.

Most people didn't respond at all and I had a few supporting public and private messages. One of the hardest responses was from a guy whom I had been friends with for years who said that "now everything had changed" when, in fact, the only change was that I was now being honest about who I was rather than hiding it.

I did have a few people representing different Christian organisations who were shocked and expressed their concerns. One organisation initially implied that I might be excommunicated from their fellowship but then realised they didn't have the authority to do so. I have tried to graciously respond to people when this happens hoping that over time their concerns would be allayed. It seems that this has mostly happened. I don't know if it will be the same when I am in a committed partnership.

It is hard for many people to understand the subtle ways in which people experience stigma and discrimination because of their sexuality. Many people believe that it is now not a problem to be gay at all. But if you asked a black person if they still experience prejudice most would say they did and still do, and I believe that it is the same for gay people. It may not be the same level as it used to be, but it is still very much there. For example, in my city, I have only ever seen gay men holding hands on Pride Day. Many gay men have told me that they would not risk holding hands in public anywhere, even in the UK. Gay men and women are still beaten up for being gay in the UK.

Over the last few years, I have come out to others when I introduce myself when I feel it is appropriate or helpful. Although society is different than it was there are still subtle forms of homophobia, particularly in many churches. Both the Catholic and Anglican church communities have recently, in some situations, allowed blessings of same-sex couples but very few churches are openly inclusive. However, this is a step forward.

I am disappointed that in my city of Swansea, which has over 60 churches, only around 4 are inclusive to LGBTQ. Sadly I think this lack of inclusivity is mainly because of the fear of losing members rather than the actual study of theology. Many would say they are too busy to have time for that, but they still have time to be homophobic.

Having done some reading on queer theology, I am now more convinced than ever that the Bible is not against homosexuality. God primarily loves everyone. Sadly, many gay Christians have labelled verses that are weaponised against them as 'Clobber' verses. One American pastor once said to me that if God really did have a problem with homosexuality then it would be way down on the list of things he had a problem with.

Another pastor in the UK told me that one man had come up to him after a service and was furious that there was a gay couple holding hands in church. The pastor told him that other sins were of much more concern and he was happy to welcome both of them to his church as he had recently led them to Christ.

Linden church, which I have been a part of for years, went through a careful process of introducing the idea of being inclusive to the congregation in the church's small groups. This gave people a chance to process it and see what scripture says rather than their beliefs being based on assumptions. Over the years Linden Church has been involved in marrying a gay couple and included teaching on, for example, understanding different sexualities and parenting gay children.

The other day a friend asked me about where I was with 'stuff'. By that he meant my sexuality. I said I was still hopeful to get a male partner. He said he thought it would be a big mistake, that I would lose all credibility on all I have achieved and people wouldn't let me near their children. He said he didn't (necessarily) believe it was wrong but that others would be upset. He said I'd managed to not have a male partner until now, so why start?

I recently got talking to a local older man who identified himself as a Christian. We both became friends when we realised we both had a strong faith, we had both been involved in mission work overseas and we had both lost our wives. But when I told him I was gay he couldn't handle it and didn't want to meet up again. He just couldn't deal with the incongruity of me being a Christian and gay.

I went to Gay Pride in my city this year and enjoyed connecting with others but I was sad that a homophobic group turned up to heckle everyone. Not a large group but enough to spoil it for some people and make other people afraid to turn up. So yes, homophobia is still alive and well.

Last year I went to Greenbelt, a Christian festival in the UK. For many years they have been inclusive providing a space for a large number of marginalised people who iden-tify as Christians, including the LGBTQ community, to feel welcome and at home. I loved it.

The Open Table Network is a growing group of communities that are providing support to Christian LGBTQ people. Their motto is "We are Equal, We are Precious. We belong".

Reflection:

The church needs to grow up and welcome their LGBTQ brothers and sisters. It is sad that in this case it is sometimes the secular community that is ahead of the Christian community in this.

Resources:

- *Green Belt* festival: greenbelt.org.uk
- *Open Table* network: opentable.lgbt

Chapter 83

Surviving the Criticism of Being a Christian

"Go slowly and go far."
Welsh Proverb

I was asked by June, my counsellor, if I could choose to be an animal what it would be. I think my animal would be a tortoise, like in the tortoise and hare fable. I am slow but I get there in the end. I had a tortoise made of cloth and all the shell squares were different colours. To me that represented different abilities rather than having one main ability. I feel like a 'jack of all trades" rather than one. But I believe that my faith is core to all I do and am.

As a child one of the reasons I think I was bullied was because I had a strong Christian faith. I knew I was loved by God and my peers considered me to be odd to believe in something invisible and to them seemed rather "silly'. I read up on Christian apologetics so I could respond to these criticisms but I wasn't very good at it.

But even as a child, I learned that people in China and

other parts of the world were being persecuted for their faith. I loved reading classic Christian books and being by heroes of faith like *'The Hiding Place'* by Corrie Ten Boom a survivor of the holocaust, *The Cross and the Switchblade* by David Wilkerson who worked with gangs in New York, and *God's Smuggler* by Brother Andrew who smuggled Bibles into Eastern Europe before the end of the cold war when it was illegal.

As I grew older I was fascinated by the strength and resilience of Christians who had survived genocide. Dietrich Bonhoeffer, a German who resisted the Nazis and was later hanged, deeply impressed me. I also read about and met several Christians who survived the Cambodian genocide including Barnabas Mam. Most Christians did not survive the genocide, neither did Muslim Immams or Buddhist Patriarchs.

One of the refugees I worked with, Sina, built a bamboo church next to the clinic in the refugee camp. When UN officials stopped their UN jeep and challenged him about it he reminded them that he had survived the persecution of Pol Pot. Was he now going to be persecuted for his faith by representatives of the United Nations? They got back in their jeep and drove away and he never heard anything more about it!

One amazing story we heard was from one of our refugee health workers who arrived in the refugee camp and saw a picture on the wall of a portrayal of Jesus. They asked who it was because they had seen him on their long trip to the border and he had led them to safety through the minefields and then disappeared. Incredible.

In the early days of being in Cambodia, we were criticised for working as we did in the slums. Some people assumed that we did it so we could 'force' people to become

Christians but mostly my experience of proselytism is that, apart from a few bad examples of cults and brainwashing, most people are not going to accept a new political or religious persuasion unless they are convinced that it is genuinely helpful to them. It is also patronising to think people can't make up their own minds. Most missionaries don't want people to be Christians just because of the benefits offered. They want people to experience the good news and love of Jesus in word and deed. The direct teachings of Jesus in the Beatitudes give instructions to us to live lives of sacrifice, non-violence, and service to everyone.

In the *Butterfly Longitudinal Research* project we found that many of the survivors had a very positive view of faith. Some remained Buddhist or returned to Buddhism. Some acquired a Christian faith and then later dropped it, but many spoke favourably of their experiences of spirituality and still do. Some spoke of how they are now encouraging others to believe. Four of the participants said that their faith had prevented them from suicide.

Over the years I have become more sceptical about some of the puritanical beliefs I grew up with. I believe, as the Quakers do, that there is something of God in everyone and that people should be encouraged to share their light with everyone. I think it is right for us to ask forgiveness for the wrong we have done but not to wallow in our sinfulness and focus on the belief that we are never good enough. I also believe that we should understand more about how evil impacts societies as a whole and consider how to challenge it rather than focusing only on the sins of individuals. I believe that communion time and Good Friday are times to reflect on our sinfulness and the rest of the time we should focus on the love of God.

So far, I have not experienced real persecution for being

a Christian and we never know how we might respond if we were put in that position. In the West, we may be mildly inconvenienced when we speak out about our faith but in many parts of the world, people are tortured and killed. Why? Because powerful governments are threatened by the alternativity of the Christian faith where people might behave in a challenging anti-authoritarian way.

I am deeply concerned with the way one current World Leader has aligned himself with Christians and even created his own version of the Bible. I also wonder whether, and when, he finally leaves if there will be a negative back-lash towards genuine Christians if it hasn't already happened.

Criticism that I have experienced is minor compared to so many others but things could change. I hope that I can be faithful to Christ when the time comes to really stand up to the challenge of persecution.

Reflection:

Open Doors says there are 365 million Christians around the world who are persecuted for their faith. That's a million people for every day of the year.

Resource:

- *Open Doors*: opendoorsuk.org

Chapter 84

Surviving Dating Applications and Sexploitation

"*For news of the heart, ask the face.*"
Cambodian Proverb

As I got more familiar with the idea of being a gay man I realised that I could explore dating. Swansea didn't seem to have many opportunities to meet people. I often felt I was "the only gay in the village" so I had to try the inevitable dating applications.

It became quickly apparent that the gay scene was very much about young beautiful bodies and not about old boys like me with 'dad bods'. Like everyone who has been on a dating app, before me, it took a bit of getting used to 'ghosting' where people, with whom you were seemingly having a nice conversation with, suddenly stop communicating!

It wasn't long before I realised that alongside people who wanted to date were quite a few scammers. The adage, "*If it seems too good to be true then it probably is*" was true! Sometimes I would be in conversation with what I thought was a handsome middle-aged chap and we seemed to be getting on well and then came the request for money. Groan. A couple of times I wanted to see where it would go and I had one request from a chap who wanted me to help him get gold bars out of a small African country but he needed money to do so! The problem with this is that I am anxious that anyone being nice is likely a scam.

On one App you were asked to pay according to the amount of time you used the App. I was surprised when many really nice guys appeared to be local and a perfect match. It took me a while to realise that it was either a bot or trained people who kept people texting so that clients spent as much time as possible on the app, so that they paid a lot of money. Indeed many apps appeared to initially be free but turned out to not be cheap at all and made their money from various additional perks. I realised that ironically I was being sexually exploited but without the sex! Funny. Not funny. Actually very disappointing when your expectations are raised and then they go nowhere.

My first real date was with a real guy who seemed real friendly and we decided to meet up. I asked him what he did for a living and he said he was a hairdresser. I asked him if he could be any more stereotypically gay. He laughed. As the time got closer, I teased him that I was concerned he might be an axe murderer. He retorted that I could be one too! Fair enough. As I got closer to the underground station we were planning to meet in, I asked him how I would recognise him. He replied that he would be the one carrying the axe! I then knew that we were going to get on fine.

We had a great time together and I found out his real passion was doing stand-up and he invited me to see him perform in his role as Elbarache, a cross between Elvis and Liberace! I was concerned that it was going to be crude but it was great fun. He got everyone up, dancing and having a good time. It didn't develop into a romantic relationship but we are still good friends.

Another date was with another hairdresser. He was thoughtful and kind. At the time I was not in a good place and I decided it wasn't going to work. I have since regretted that decision but it is too late now.

Another dating connection was with a handsome Dutch fellow. He had a really interesting background having been an Olympian in beach volleyball. He also previously worked as a cabin crew for various airlines and as a barman on the Orient Express. He had leukaemia but it hadn't stopped him from being an elite athlete. He later moved to Italy and continues to train newcomers in beach volleyball. I visited him there and we remain friends.

I had one guy contact me through a dating App that said he knew me! Apparently we had been in the same church youth group many years before. We seemed to have a lot in common so we agreed to meet up in Swansea. When he arrived he embarrassed me by kissing me in the street before we had even got inside. The rest of the weekend was a blur but it involved a lot of snogging. But after he had left and the hormones had subsided I realised that I didn't really like him. When I contacted him he was understandably upset. All I could do was apologise.

I had one date with a guy but it was clear to me that there wasn't chemistry for something more. He must have complained to the App who then removed me from their clients. I tried to argue with the App staff that I had not said or done anything inappropriate and asked them to check, but they weren't interested in anything I had to say and I continued to be banned.

I also was sent an email from Christian Connection.

Although I was impressed they would accept applications from gay men, I was less than impressed when they sent me a note saying I had been banned. When I questioned it they said that they needed more information on who I was which I understood, but it was rather alarmist to be banned without what I felt was an adequate explanation. I also decided not to re-apply because there were only about 15 gay men on their App! A friend suggested that for my notoriety I should get a T-shirt that said 'I was banned from the Christian Connection App!'.

I wanted to find someone of faith and spirituality but finding someone who hadn't been badly wounded by the church or who had kept their faith despite being that was hard. Some friends introduced me to a lovely guy who was a retired vicar and we immediately hit it off. I thought that it was going to develop into a serious relationship but after a couple of dates he contacted me and I got the *'Dear John'* e-mail. Even though we only met up a few times I was heartbroken.

I recently met a lovely guy on a Christian dating App who had a fascinating background working on ships as a navigator. We are currently friends.

Reflection:

I can only do the hard work of online dating once in a while. It's exhausting. JFYI I would prefer to be introduced by friends. Suggestions on a postcard...

Resources:

- *RAINN* Tips for safer online dating: <u>rainn.org/articles/tips-safer-online-dating-and-dating-app-use</u>
- Reporting Sexploitation - *Internet Watch Foundation*: <u>iwf.org.uk</u>

Chapter 85

Surviving Being a Reluctant LGBTQ Advocate in Ethiopia

"A cactus tastes bitter only to those who taste it."
Ethiopian proverb

So over the years I have been training from a Diploma up to a Ph.D. level in Holistic Child Development, which effectively means anything involving children in difficult circumstances around the world. I have visited Ethiopia three times to teach the Masters in Holistic Child Development (HCD) course.

I was recently in Addis Ababa speaking on their Masters level course. When I was walking outside of the campus, two men approached me. One pushed me onto the back of the other who was crouching down and they tried to grab my phone/wallet and run off in different directions. Fortunately, they didn't succeed. I ran after one shouting but, of course, I didn't catch him and wouldn't have known what to do if I had! It left me feeling unsettled.

I usually train in child safeguarding and child participation. One of the challenging parts of this training in the developing world is often corporal punishment. Even though it can be controversial I think it is important for students at this level to understand that there are different positions in the church on this issue.

Whilst some conservative Christians continue to believe the importance of beating their child to discipline them, others believe the Bible offers a non-violent alternative. People who support the former view don't like it to be called 'violent' but if the same level of violence was used on adults it would be considered 'grievous bodily harm' (GBH). I know some parents genuinely believe that if they don't use corporal punishment they could harm their children. However, I think the majority of parents (including myself) have used violence in discipline, not because they believe it is mandatory, but because they lose control of their anger and take it out on their children. Learning about alternative methods of discipline is vital.

Teaching about this in Ethiopia I was surprised that some of the students were so adamant that corporal punishment should be used. I tried to provide an alternative understanding of scripture from Psalm 23 where the rod is a shepherd's hook, used to guide and rescue the sheep, rather than beat them. The overall emphasis of scripture in disciplining children is love and nurturing and not extracting sin through punishment. I think this idea is a fundamental understanding for those working as advocates for children.

I also know from research that children who experience corporal punishment as children are more likely to go on to experience other forms of violence and exploitation. This is because of a phenomenon known as 'learned helplessness'. It becomes harder for them to defend and protect themselves from other forms of harm as they lose confidence in themselves and their ability to protect themselves.

In our discussions, we got on to the topic of sexuality. This created some tension in the room but as it was a Master's level course I felt that it was important for the class to hear perspectives that were maybe different from the ones that they were used to. It became apparent that the group primarily had one perspective and it was anti-gay.

As far as the group was concerned, being gay was wrong and incomprehensible as a Christian. I shared my understanding of the story of the Ethiopian eunuch in the Acts of the Apostles which was relevant as everyone in the room was Ethiopian. I believe that God went to some trouble to ensure that the eunuch heard the gospel. As a result the eunuch could be baptised so that another group of people who were marginalised could feel welcome into God's Kingdom. I didn't want to add more tension in the room by admitting that I was gay but I emphasised that I felt that there needed to be a more compassionate stance.

At one point I decided we needed to move on to discuss other things but the group said they wanted us to continue discussing it. So we did. What I didn't know was that someone was audio-recording what I said. The class finished and I returned to the missionary guesthouse.

The next morning the Dean came to the guesthouse before I was due to travel to the seminary. He told me that the police had come to the seminary early to discuss what I had been teaching. They had got hold of the audio recording and were not happy with what was being taught. The Dean said they would deal with it. So I was told not to return to the seminary but rather to change my flight so I could leave that day. I was deeply distressed about the potential outcomes for the seminary as well as being anxious for my safety. I managed to get the last flight out and arrived at the airport early. After I had checked in I was asked to sit by the gate whilst everyone else boarded. No explanation was given but I felt that the police may have told the airline to do it in order to intimidate me.

This experience made me realise just how hard it is for people in countries where it is illegal to be gay. I had a tiny taste of threat and this feeling didn't leave me for several weeks.

Reflection:

It is hard for people to understand something unless they have been through it. As the proverb says, *"A cactus tastes bitter only to those who taste it"*. It is easy for people to label someone a sinner who doesn't struggle or isn't likely to ever struggle with the same issue.

Resources:

- Books:

1. *The Queer Bible Commentary* Edited by Deryn Guest et. al SCM Press 1988.
2. *Christianity, Social Tolerance and Homosexuality* by John Boswell University of Chicago Press. 1982.
3. *UnConditional: Rescuing the Gospel from the Gays-vs-Christians* debate by Justin Lee. Hodder & Stoughton 2013
4. *A Life of Unlearning; A preacher's struggle with his homosexuality, church and faith* by Anthony Venn-Brown. Lightning Source. 2015

- *All Out*: Campaigning for global equality for LGBTQ where discrimination is challenged: allout.org/en

Glenn Miles PhD

Or scan me instead!

Chapter 86

Surviving Depression, Vicarious Trauma and Post Traumatic Stress Disorder

"Tapping persistently breaks the stone."
Welsh Proverb

R ecent research indicates that people with head trauma are four times more likely to suffer from depression afterwards than those who have not had a head injury. After we came back from Cambodia following the head injury we had lost everything that was important to us apart from each other. It certainly drew us together but I admit to getting quite depressed.

After the head injury we had very little money, we were living in a basement flat, I had lost a dynamic, interesting job, and I was effectively disabled with headaches and poor balance. We had lost our first baby. We were told not to apply for disability allowance because it might go against us when Siobhan applied for a visa. I did manage to get some counselling from the hospital but it was limited. At that time they mainly thought PTSD happened to soldiers but it also happens to people working with traumatised people too.

When we were later working in Cambodia with Love 146 I got very distressed with the challenges of managing a team with what I saw as little support from the home office. So I started taking antidepressants. I think it helped but there are plenty of Christians who feel that you should just trust God and not rely on help of this kind. I disagree, especially where you are expected to carry more than the normal amount of challenges.

I believe that life is so complex and difficult at times, sometimes we experience a level of trauma, anxiety and/or depression where we need additional help for a while. I did pray and I did seek to share with friends, but even that wasn't enough.

There have been times when I have been in tears with what I have seen or even read about in the research we do with vulnerable children and others. This is vicarious trauma. I have sometimes felt hopeless to do anything of substance to address their needs. Other times I have felt that the gifts I have been given have enabled me to make a difference in the life of a person or community. It has always been very up and down and not an upward trajectory as we would all prefer. This is why so many people are only able to work in this area for a limited time or we move into something less 'in your face'.

My parents were very caring over this time and we were always welcome to their home. I regret now that I believed the popular Christian psychology such as what was written by Leanne Payne that suggested your parents make you gay from the way they bring you up. Even though I did love them it created a rift between us as I felt they were somehow responsible, which was unhelpful and untrue.

Reflection:

There have been other times when the traumas of the past come back at me and slap me around the face with nightmares and unpleasant deja vu. Being sexually abused as a child, the head injury and Siobhan's miscarriage, Siobhan's complicated pregnancies and cancer, Siobhan dying, someone close to me being raped, being fired, and coming out as a gay man. Also the challenges around Teddy's birth and Sarah's major surgery. These things are not quickly resolved. I sometimes wonder why they call it post-traumatic stress disorder as I am still waiting for the 'post' bit!

Resources:

- Vicarious Trauma: bma.org.uk/advice-and-support/your-wellbeing/vicarious-trauma/vicarious-trauma-signs-and-strategies-for-coping
- Post-Traumatic Stress Disorder: nhs.uk/mental-health/conditions/post-traumatic-stress-disorder-ptsd/symptoms/

Chapter 87

Surviving Suicidal Ideation

"Suicide is not an answer, it's destruction."
Al Green

Suicide is a terrible thing even to consider. But the reality is that many people do consider it even if they don't go through with it. I have thought and dreamed about suicide on several occasions. It is usually when I have experienced a series of hardships and there seems to be no letup.

It is hard for people to understand just how conflicting it is for a young Christian to have a same-sex attraction in a church environment where you are subtly being indoctrinated with the idea that who you are is fundamentally wrong. You feel that you are forced to choose between being a Christian or being gay.

At some level, you believe that God loves you but the incongruity can be too difficult. For some people, the discrimination and stigma they experience leads them to leave the church and never look back. For others, they feel they need to concede to trying to live a celibate life, even though this feels an impossibility. For some, they feel that suicide is the only answer.

For those coming out later in life, the choice is also challenging. Churches would prefer that you keep quiet than be open about who you really are. So they are effectively telling you lying is better than telling the truth. It's embarrassing for the church to have someone who was respected in the church to come out so it's easier to reject them.

My friend Steve G. in Cambodia committed suicide. It was not about his sexuality. It was carefully planned over many months. He was deeply depressed but none of his friends realised that it was as serious as it was. After he did it, he left many people wondering if they could have done something to prevent it.

A relative recently attempted suicide. They believed that they were saved from death for a reason but they are left with very serious consequences. Another close relative often refers to suicide, talking about it flippantly as if it is an inevitability. This way of talking is, of course, a call for help and when I hear it I am alerted to listen to what else is being said.

According to CDCP, suicide is the second leading cause of death among young people aged 10 to 14, and the third leading cause of death among 15-24 year-olds (Centers for Disease Control and Prevention, 2022). Lesbian, gay, bisexual, transgender, queer, and questioning (LGBTQ+) young people are more than four times as likely to attempt suicide than their peers (Johns et al., 2020).

Glenn Miles PhD

Reflection:

The church must not contribute to the stressors that young LGBTQ experience. They should be the ones who are welcoming, supporting and loving of the LGBTQ community.

Resource:

- *The Trevor Project*: <u>thetrevorproject.org/re-sources/article/facts-about-lgbtq-youth-suicide</u>

Chapter 88

Surviving Titles – Good and Bad

"You can't sit in a basket and lift it up yourself."
(Don't brag about yourself)
Cambodian Proverb

My full letters are Glenn Miles PhD (UW-Swansea), MSc. (UCL-ICH), PGCE-PCET (TStD, Swansea) FRCPH, FHEA, RGN (KCL-STH), RSCN (KCL-GH), RN (California) Cert Trop Med (LSTM). All these letters may look impressive and they represent a lot of work. I know I am a bit of a show off but if I can't put them in my autobiography...

It is surprising how many ways you can spell Glenn. Glen, Glyn, Glyneth, Glynn. Some people still spell me with one n when it is on the text and email so I respond by adding an n to my email or text back Glennn. One person genuinely thought that I was choosing to change my name to Glennn with 3 n's.

Although I have only held one passport whilst the rest of the family have had 2 or even 3, I have lived in Wales for around 12 years so I consider myself partly Welsh as apparently you are allowed to play rugby after living in Wales for 4 years!

Over the years I had many titles and names. Globule, Eugene, and Glumglows were my affectionate childhood nicknames alongside the less kind Glenda, Poofta, and Wa*ker.

When I worked as a camp counsellor in the States I was Counselor Glenn. Then I was a Student Nurse and then Staff Nurse Miles.

Working in the refugee camps, my call sign was Bravo 2.

When I started working overseas I was called a missionary by some and a development worker by others. Although missionary is in our current Western culture seen as a derogatory term I did/do believe that I was called by God to spread the good news of Jesus. If you are not sure what I mean by that, then read the Beatitudes in Matthew and one of the gospels. You will be challenged! I recently spoke to a guy on a plane and suggested to him that he read the Beatitudes. We kept in touch and he said he was deeply moved by what he read.

I considered that doing justice work for God was missionary work but others considered that *real* mission involved evangelical conversion although sometimes people in Asia have/do call me Pastor. I am not ashamed to be called a Christian but I have been ashamed of what fellow Christians have done and said in the name of Jesus. I am also proud of what many of my Christian friends have done.

Early in my career, I signed up to a program where you got University credit for relevant work you had done. I got references from people I had worked with in all my previous jobs. I submitted everything and was thrilled to receive a Bachelors in Health Administration. I later found out that it was a scam.

Pronouns are important to some. I identify as a he/him.

In Pakistan I was called Gulab Chund (which means Rose Moon). Isn't it interesting that in our culture Rose is a feminine name but in Pakistan, it is a masculine name!

In Asia, my name has been mistakenly pronounced Mr. Glans (!) or Mr. Glean (!). As I got involved in lecturing and teaching in various seminaries and conferences before and after getting my Ph.D., sometimes people called me Dr. Glenn or Professor Miles. Like many researchers it took me a while to own the title of *doctor,* feeling a sense of imposter's syndrome to be called anything so lofty.

I have the title of an *author* and an *editor* which are both equally challenging roles. People often think an editor just means collecting other people's papers and pasting them together but it is much more challenging than that!

I have been called an *Abolitionist* in both a positive and negative way. I am well aware that some have seen me as a 'white saviour' but I try hard not to be. If being colonial is patronising, I admit that there have been times when I might have been a bit more colonial than I should have been.

I was recently called an *Original Gangster* which I thought was wonderful. I think it basically means an advocate of age.

I have tried to be an *advocate* for people without a voice, especially children, but I have recognised my whole career that children and vulnerable adults should ideally be listened to and supported to be their own advocates where possible. So in research reports when I can I use children's voices in quotes as it is often much more powerful than statistics as they provide a sense of reality and authenticity

I used to want to have darker skin so that I could be

considered on an equal footing with my peers in developing countries but apart from a suntan that hasn't happened!

I was given the title of Fellow on two occasions. *Fellow of the Royal College of Public Health* for my work in public health and *Fellow of the Higher Education Authority* for my work in providing education for people in the higher education sector. I am particularly proud of the latter because the first time I was turned down but they personally requested me to provide them with the information they required for me to achieve it.

Having a PhD has allowed me to speak on *Capitol Hill* in Washington DC, the *Houses of Parliament* in London and the *Cambodian Senate* in Phnom Penh. It has opened doors I would not otherwise have been offered and I am grateful for those opportunities.

Over the years I have been fortunate to be called son, brother, uncle, grandson, husband, dad and grandad.

Then, of course, you can buy a nobility title from about ten pounds to several thousand! I could dress up as Lord (or Lady!) Such and such but I probably wouldn't go outside the house!

As Siobhan and my daughters have become increasingly well known and established in their own right, I was called by Siobhan's partner (and later widow) and more recently Zoe/Hannah/Sarah's father/dad/daddy. But my favourite title is Granddad or Grandps or Bampi by my grandson Teddy.

Reflection:

It's never a good idea to brag about yourself but I feel like I have enough people who ensure that my ego is kept in check. However, I actually think that it isn't a bad thing to celebrate the achievements of others and even of yourself. As long as you remember you can't take it with you. I still have Siobhan's hard-earned certificates of all her degrees but they are, of course, worth nothing now.

Resource:

- Buy your nobility title: <u>nobility.co.uk</u>

Chapter 89

Surviving Developing Pioneering Organisations and Projects

"It always seems impossible until it's done."
Nelson Mandela

O ver the years I have had the privilege of pioneering a number of NGOs and projects. Pioneering is not always easy. Like in the Biblical story of Nehemiah, there is often opposition, misunderstandings and jealousy. I also believe that breaking new ground in the justice area requires much spiritual warfare and prayer.

I have been grateful over the years for having many people praying for the work I have done:

1. The first project I started was *Servants to Asia's Urban Poor Cambodia, an NGO* whose intention was to live in the slum areas in Phnom Penh. Siobhan and I were the co-leaders. We set up 3 projects; 1) working with children

impacted by HIV/AIDS 2) working with slum children in malnutrition clinics 3) working with children with disabilities.

2. The next project I started was *Parents and Professionals Resource Information Centre Access (PAPRICA)*, a centre for parents and professionals working with children with special needs in Lambeth, South London. It was after my head injury and I enjoyed doing something practical again.

3. I worked with *Tearfund UK* as the Children at Risk Facilitator in Cambodia identifying projects with the emerging church that Tearfund could fund and I could capacity build with. I co-authored the Tearfund *Children at Risk Guidelines* with Paul Stephenson.

4. I co-edited the Celebrating Children book with Jo- Joy Wright published by *Paternoster/Authentic Media* and ran the first *Celebrating Children* course in Cambodia. I also co-wrote the *Celebrating Children* workbooks for *Viva Equip.*

5. The *EFC Children's Commission* was started with Thong Romanea when I was working with Tearfund. The initial purpose was to train people using the *Celebrating Children* curriculum developed by *Viva.* The first year we had 60 child care workers from NGOs and Churches. We wanted to encourage the church to understand that children were God's priority.

6. *Chab Dai* (Hands Together) is an anti-trafficking network started by Helen Sworn and myself. Originally it was based in Cambodia

only but over the years it has been involved in helping many anti-trafficking networks around the world. The purpose of the network is to learn and collaborate together and share resources.

7. *Care for the Elderly*- Swansea is a small branch of an organisation that provides a hot drink and a slice of cake for lonely elderly folk once a month on a Sunday afternoon. I set it up in between the times we lived in Cambodia but I believe it is still going on.

8. The Flipbooks project is a project that creates anti-trafficking toolkits for children at risk of trafficking and other challenges. It was started under *Chab Dai* but is now in two parts. I facilitate the Asia program with the *up! Collective* and Sam and Hannah of *Tehila* develop flipbooks in Zambia. We have Flipbooks addressing appropriate and inappropriate touch for children, children accessing porn, children being groomed for sexual exploitation, and for refugee children coming to a new country. New ones are being developed to address bullying, period poverty and anxiety & depression.

9. I started *Love 146* in Cambodia in 2009. We helped do capacity building and funding of small anti-trafficking organisations. We also did a series of research projects in Cambodia, Thailand and the Philippines with young men, street boys and transgender.

10. I facilitated a number of interns to work with *Love 146* on local research projects. For some

they were part of an academic programme. For others it enabled them to work with a team on designing, conducting, analysing and presenting research and then doing an initial report. Many went on to do significant work in justice.

11. The *Men & the Sex Trade* project in Cambodia which became the *GLU* (Guys Like Us!) project in Cambodia with the *Message Parlour* in the red light area for male sex buyers. This was with John Y.

12. The *Chab Dai* Butterfly Longitudinal Research Project (BLRP) was started with Siobhan with a research team, which followed survivors of sex trafficking for ten years. I helped Siobhan in the early stages and helped to tie things up at the end with James.

13. I have facilitated a series of research projects on the vulnerabilities of sexual exploitation of young men and boys in Asia with Jarrett Davis. We started this project with *Love146* and finished it with up! International. This expanded to include street children and transgender as well.

14. I also led a research project with *Love146* in Cambodia with our interns who interviewed both expat and local sex buyers of women and men, also with the help of James.

15. I co-edited a series of three books on a Christian response to Human Trafficking for *Regnum Publishers* in Oxford with Christa Crawford. 'Stopping the Traffick: A Christian Response to Sexual Exploitation & Trafficking' (Regnum 2014), Finding our Way Through the Traffick:

Navigating our way through the complexities of a Christian response to sexual exploitation and Human Trafficking' (Regnum 2017) and 'Stepping out of the Traffick: Pausing for theological reflection on a Christian response to sexual exploitation and trafficking' (Regnum 2024 All available from www.ocms.ac.uk/regnum as well as Amazon.

16. Over COVID I started the *Abolitionist Book Club* (*ABC*) which provided weekly, bi-weekly and then monthly Zoom meetings where we discussed research around sexual exploitation and trafficking from various perspectives. People would be encouraged to read between one and three open-access research papers and then we would discuss them in the meeting.

17. I am in the process of pioneering a series of research projects listening to survivors for the *Journal of Human Trafficking* on 'Survivor Voices' in Cambodia, the USA and the Netherlands...

18. I conducted anonymous research with Christian missionaries and development workers in Cambodia on sexual behaviour they had experienced. I am currently leading research with Christian men in Europe. We have completed research in the UK and Germany and hope to do it in Portugal and the Czech Republic this coming year.

19. As well as supervising several PhD students; Sheryl (Albania), Maryan (England), Carrissa (USA >South Africa), Bishnu (Nepal), William (Kenya), I have/am also supervised others

wanting to do research in their contexts as a stepping stone to doing a research degree and others simply to be able to do research to advocate; Bandara, (Sri Lanka), Matt (Kurdish refugees), Nicole (Mexico), Becky (London), Vincent (Netherlands), Adrian (Australia).

20. I am on the board of the newly formed network the *International Coalition Against Modern Slavery*.

Reflection:

Writing these out I had no idea there would be so much and realised that I can be proud of what I have achieved and not squirm behind my Britishness

Resources:

- My personal website also has much of our research and training: gmmiles.co.uk
- *Asia Pacific Nazarene Theological Seminary Holistic Child Development* PhD programme: apnts.edu.ph/

Or scan me instead!

Chapter 90

Surviving Leaving Badly vs. Leaving Well

"If there is no struggle, there is no progress."
Cambodian Proverb

I often thought that the diverse and varied ways that we left Cambodia/Thailand should be published for people care on different classic ways to leave *or not leave* your assignment:

1. **Leaving my work with the U.N. refugee camp** and youth with a mission to get married has got to be pretty high up there for nice ways to leave. The refugees were being repatriated back to Cambodia. We initially went to the UK for Siobhan to meet my parents in person. I then did a short course while Siobhan flew home to deal with the final arrangements for our beautiful wedding. We later returned to the team in Thailand who

were just winding up before closing the program. Nice exit. We felt God was really looking after us.

2. **Leaving from Servants with 'the serious head injury',** Siobhan and I had/have the reputation for having the most dramatic exit ever from Cambodia. People were still talking about it when we returned to live there seven years after we had left! The people management was disastrous. We were living in a war zone. There were no good medical facilities. There were no medical evacuation possibilities. And yet we felt God was really looking after us in the details.

3. **With Tearfund I had a contract, and I completed my contract.** We prepared to go. I handed over responsibilities which I had prepared for months in advance. We left. I had a good debriefing. Doesn't that sound nice? I recommend this way! We felt God was really looking after us.

4. **Being unexpectedly and suddenly asked to leave from Love146** was very painful and it was handled very badly. There was no need for the sudden exit. The organisation was going in a different direction from us but they had not communicated anything with us. Then they blamed me for causing them to not achieve a merger which was simply not true. I made mistakes but I was not the man they made me out to be. It was a covenant way to dispense of me. The result? Messiness. Confusion, Hurt. Anger, not just us

either. Incomplete work. Reputation loss. And yet we felt God was really looking after us

Debriefing after leaving well, or badly, was really important. Churches can be very helpful but they don't always understand the challenges of re-integrating cross-culturally back home after a time away, especially when you have worked in a traumatic context. We were grateful to an organisation La Rucher close to Geneva who provided excellent resources to help us and others adjust.

Reflection:

When it is time for me to leave this earth as it is, although I do hope for a new Earth, I hope that I can leave well. It has been quite an adventure but I couldn't have done it without God by my side and my family and friends.

Resource:

- *La Rucher*: lerucher.org

Chapter 91

Surviving Organised Criminal Gangs

"Seeing a tiger sleep, you assume the tiger is dead; seeing a tiger crouch, you assume the tiger is kneeling."
(Things are not necessarily as you perceive them to be)
Unkown

I have been invited to help several groups of people to help them have their voices heard:

1. A group of survivors of human trafficking through the Global Association of Human Trafficking Scholars who want to do research on Survivor Leaders.
2. The survivors of the Butterfly research who have made recommendations to NGOs, police and commune leaders.
3. A group of survivors of human trafficking in Cambodia who want to represent their community to advocate for them.

4. A group of survivors of cleric abuse (sexual abuse by church leaders) who want to use their voice to help prevent it from happening to others

5. A group of survivors of criminal gang sadistic child sexual exploitation who are now adults who want their voices to be heard.

Criminal exploitation is another example of the worst form of humanity where people are exploited, tortured and sold. A very real threat that can continue for child survivors of this type of violence into their adulthood.

The process of listening to survivors can be long as they decide if they can trust you and work out what they are willing to share. The ethics of doing this kind of research is also complicated. I feel that this kind of work needs the prayer support of a team of people. Please join us in this task.

I have been told that doing this kind of research could go against me. The gangs could find ways to discredit me and my work. They could threaten me as well. We haven't got to that stage yet but I realise it is a very real threat. I believe God is with me in everything but I know his protection doesn't mean I am cushioned in a bubble where there is no risk of harm...

I know 5 is of what might be ahead (I hope not) rather than what's happened – so it's a story of being willing to face the possibility of having to face and survive this in the future.

Reflection:

I feel enormously privileged to be asked to help people find their voices to help others. I hope I can be brave enough to rise to the task.

Resource:

- Dangers of criminal exploitation: nspcc.org.uk/what-is-child-abuse/types-of-abuse/gangs-criminal-exploitation

Chapter 92

Surviving Victimhood

"You can't go back and change the beginning, but you can start where you are and change the ending."
C.S. Lewis

Being a survivor we need to be careful that we don't wallow in victimhood but look to the positivity of survivorhood! We can be proud of our resilience. These are some of the lessons I have learnt from being a survivor not in any particular order:

1. God loves you more than you could imagine. He loves everyone, even people you don't.
2. Understanding God's grace is the most important thing you can do.
3. Always try to listen more than you talk.
4. Live generously with your time as well as your money.

5. Greet people and smile, even if they don't return the greeting.
6. Tell people especially friends you appreciate/love them and why.
7. If you want to, wear bright colours and clothes or even drag. Do it and accept compliments when people say nice things to you.
8. Always be open to learning and don't be afraid to question things you have always considered to be true. Remain curious.
9. Thank everyone who serves you. Be thankful to God too.
10. Appreciate the health you have. Remain hopeful for healing for any illness you have.
11. Look for honest mentors to guide you. Look out for people you yourself can mentor and guide.
12. Family is priority. Keep hold of them. But if they keep hurting you, hold them at arm's length.
13. Learn to forgive better those who hurt you.
14. Love is love.
15. If it is hurtful to stay in your church they are doing it wrong. Go to another church.
16. Learn to understand the true meaning of God's Grace and live in it.
17. Survivors understand survivors. Find peers who get you.
18. Get a hobby you enjoy and commit some time to doing it.
19. Don't feel guilty when you sleep or rest. Rest often when you are able.
20. Count your blessings every day. Especially the days you find it hard to find them.

21. Communication with your children is more important than doing things that they might perceive as interference.
22. You will never find a perfect church. Help make your one better unless 13.
23. Be kind to yourself
24. Friends are important for survival. Hold on to them. If you lose them, find new ones even if it feels hard to do so.

Reflection:

It's not helpful to dwell on being a victim but you still need time to process trauma.

Resource:

- Survivor vs. Victim - language challenges: <u>rsacc-thecentre.org.uk/guest-blogs/victim-survivor-the-importance-of-the-language-we-use-to-talk-about-people-who-have-experienced-sexual-violence</u>

Chapter 93

Surviving the Church

"And let us consider how to stir up one another to love and good works."
Hebrews 10:24

The global church is the largest social welfare organisation in the world and it has the potential to make a difference like no Government or Organisation. But it needs the courage to step into the darkness carrying the light of God.

The church can be a wonderful place of community where people experience God's love and healing, or it can be a place where people feel judged and are made to feel the heavy weight of sinfulness. I am not saying that people shouldn't recognise their sins and be genuinely sorry but to be reminded week after week after week is wearying, shameful and ultimately traumatic as you feel constantly unworthy, even when you may have little to be sorry about.

I believe the story of the cross is redemption at both an

individual and societal level. When Jesus talks about the Kingdom of God he is talking about how things can be transformed in this life rather than focusing on the after-life. Practical Theology looks very different when you use this lens. It becomes more hopeful rather than giving up on the now. We also need to recognise that doing justice is what we are all called to do, not just a ministry on the side.

In research we did in Cambodia we found that people who had been sexually exploited experienced prejudice from leaders in the church. Many had discovered a new faith but were turned away by the church. I doubt it would be much different in my country.

So, if I would dare assume I have the right to, what would I recommend to the church?

First there are some amazing Christians who do some amazing things with God's help. But the church in the Minority North (West) must change to be relevant to society and a world which is, in many ways, falling apart:

1. All churches must welcome everyone.
   Exclusion is unbiblical. Churches need to consider where they are excluding people, intentionally or unintentionally and seek to rectify it. This includes people LGBTQ and those with disabilities.
2. All churches must have safeguarding policies to guard vulnerable people from ourselves and unscrupulous others
3. All churches must emphasise the love of God more than the weight of sin.
4. All churches must challenge injustice locally and globally.

5. All churches must challenge their own Pharisiacalness.
6. All churches must encourage people to love God and be kind to others.
7. A united church is a strong church. Churches should seek opportunities to work together
8. The church needs to address pornography, and sexual behaviour that harms others by people in the church
9. The church must recognise the enormous gap between the wealth of the North and the poverty of the South and be sacrificially generous in its giving.
10. The church must not be fatalistic in its attitude to the end of the world but look for ways to protect the earth, its flora and fauna and the most vulnerable.

Reflection:

Churches need to learn to be open to change even though change can be hard.

Resources:

- *Tearfund* is involved in supporting the church worldwide to do justice: tearfund.org
- *Chab Dai* is involved in helping anti-trafficking organisations to learn and work together: chabddai.org
- Safeguarding in Churches: thirtyoneeight.org/help-and-resources/publications
- Safeguarding in Faith Based Organisations and other Non-Government Organisations: keepingchildrensafe.global/resources
- Our research on the Cambodian church's prejudice against formerly exploited women: digitalcommons.uri.edu/dignity/vol5/iss1/4
- *up! International* is the organisation I am linked to. We are involved in doing research with grassroots organisations to help those working at the coalface to better understand the context and therefore work more effectively: up-international.org

Chapter 94

Thriving with Jesus

"When you saw only one set of footprints, it was then that I carried you."
Footsteps in the Sand by Ryan Hart

J esus is my hero. I know he loves me unconditionally. I know he has carried me and still carries me through the hardest times. The concept of grace and God's unimaginably deep love for me has carried me through the darkest times. I have felt the true meaning of Cwyth when I imagine being cwyth-ed by Jesus.

I recently went to see a performance of *Jesus Christ Superstar* with my daughters at the local Swansea Arena. It was an amazing performance. But the week before I had a nasty chest infection and didn't think I would make it right up to a few hours before the performance. I was delighted to let my friends know that "I had seen *Jesus!*" Hooray.

Some time ago I was commissioned by the *Lausanne Committee on Children at Risk* to create a toolkit to help people working with children to understand the biblical foundation for why it is important for us to listen to and involve children in programs and planning (child participation). Some people think that child participation is just a fad and that it does not have a theological basis. I disagree and believe that it is fundamental to our understanding of a Christian approach to child development. Children must be respected for what they can contribute.

I was able to work with my friend Andre, a brilliant community animator, on this toolkit and I am very excited about the potential it has. The actual process of working with a team of theologians and practitioners to create it wasn't always easy for us but I think our friendships became stronger as a result. The result is an anime flipbook suitable for older children and their teachers. We are working with a different creator of animations to use the same pictures but create them to be more suitable for younger children.

After Siobhan died a friend, who has no faith that I am aware of, said to me after the memorial service that they knew I was a Christian and that it was important to me, but if I needed to talk he was there. I think they saw Jesus as a kind of crutch with limits to how much it is able to hold you up. In the end I am grateful for friends like him who cared but I am grateful for a God who I believe loves me beyond measure.

I have recently very much enjoyed watching the series called *The Chosen (Angel Studios)*. It has been developed by a broad church of Christians and they have sought the help of theologians to be sure that it is accurate culturally and theologically. Rather than a 90-minute film it has been made in several series of episodes. This gives it time to develop the characters of the disciples as well as other characters - the centurion, the Pharisees, and Mary Magdalene.

It is well worth watching. I am aware that some people may feel it is 'liberal' but I don't believe this to be true.

I have also enjoyed listening to the daily devotions on the *Lectio 365 App*. I love listening to it and it sets me up for the day. Every day the devotion finishes with this prayer;

Father, help me to live this day to the full, being true to You, in every way.

Jesus, help me to give myself away to others, being kind to everyone I meet.

Spirit, help me to love the lost, proclaiming Christ in all I do and say.

Amen.

A good friend who very much considered himself to be a Christian recently told me that he had changed his opinion and thought that it all (Christianity) seemed very silly so he could no longer believe it to be true. This made me sad for him but did make me consider what he was saying instead of just accepting it because I had done so forever. Why do we take this bronze age community so seriously and a story about a man Jesus who died 2000 years ago?

A Life Lived

In the tapestry of life, a tale unfolds,
A story of resilience, of strength and of courage,
Of a soul who has faced trials and storms,
Yet stands strong, rooted in love and knowledge.
At fourteen, a boy, innocence stolen away,

The pain of abuse, a wound deep and raw,
Yet, within the darkness, a spark of hope,
A resilience born, a will to explore and
    know.
A nurse in training, a heart called to care,
A tender touch, a gentle smile, a comforting
    voice,
In the midst of suffering, a beacon of light,
A purpose revealed, a calling to give a
    choice.
A refugee camp, a world unseen,
A crisis-torn land, a people in need,
A tender heart, a fierce defender,
A witness to the beauty of humanity's will to
    succeed.
A union of hearts, a love that transcends,
A journey to Cambodia, a life rearranged,
A family born, a love that grows,
A dance of love, a partnership engaged.
Trauma and loss, a head injury severe,
A life at risk, a family in fear,
Yet, through the darkness, a light emerges,
A love that holds, a strength that's clear.
Two children born, a dance of life,
A journey of love, a family's delight,
A bond unbroken, a future assured,
A love that transcends, a hope that takes
    flight.
A doctorate earned, a knowledge gained,
A journey of discovery, a passion ignited,
A focus on trafficking, a pursuit of justice,
A life lived in love, a legacy brightened.
A director of an NGO, a vision to share,

Glenn Miles PhD

A heart for the children, a voice for the
  oppressed,
A legacy of love, a path to follow,
A journey of hope, a future blessed.
A dismissal, a challenge, a storm to weather,
A resilience born, a strength to rely,
A will to continue, a love that sustains,
A journey of faith, a love that won't die.
A diagnosis, a challenge, a storm to weather,
A resilience born, a strength to rely,
A will to continue, a love that sustains,
A journey of faith, a love that won't die.
A loss, a heartache, a storm to weather,
A resilience born, a strength to rely,
A will to continue, a love that sustains,
A journey of faith, a love that won't die.
A coming out, a truth to embrace,
A journey of self-discovery, a love that's true,
A legacy of love, a life that's blessed,
A journey of faith, a love that's pursued.
A grandson born, a family's joy,
A love that transcends, a legacy bright,
A journey of love, a future assured,
A love that endures, a light that's bright.
A journey of faith, a God that's true,
A love that sustains, a grace that's free,
A life lived in love, a hope that's secure,
A legacy of love, a legacy that's me.
So, dear friend, in the midst of the storm,
Seek God's love, a refuge in the night,
A hope that endures, a love that's true,
A journey of faith, a life that's bright.

Embracing (Cwtch-ing) Me, God and Others!

Reflection:

It's hard to explain a love to and from Jesus when others can see nothing except the fruits of it in your life. We recently had an exercise in my church where people wrote on a card the impact their relationship with Jesus had on their lives. The responses were extraordinary. You should try it!

Resources:

- *The Jesus Toolkit* – developed by Glenn Miles and Andre Van Wyk: gmmiles.co.uk/wp-content/uploads/2021/01/Jesus-Toolkit-Colour-condensed.pptx
- *The Chosen*: thechosen.tv/e
- Lectio 365: 24-7prayer.com/resource/lectio-365.

Chapter 95

What's Next?

"And we know that in all things God works for the good of those who love him, who have been called according to his purpose."
Romans 8:28

It is almost exactly 50 years since I was sexually abused by a man in a Christian conference centre in England. I have had to mostly keep it silent for all that time. In addition, I have hidden the fact that I am a gay man. It is time to break the silence for me and for others.

Mumbles is a delightful village on the outskirts of Swansea city. I have lived in the area for a total of 13 years over two periods. A number of challenging things happened over that time but I am grateful to have lived in such a beautiful part of Wales. Who wouldn't enjoy living on the coastline with a view of the constantly changing views of the sea and tides, and a lighthouse out of your bedroom window?

And yet, having had such a busy active international

life, it is not always easy to be in a place that can be quite parochial. I am grateful that I am still able to travel.

I first moved into the place I now live to make room for the Ukrainian refugee family. Barbara was happy to let me use the top room with the view but it didn't have central heating and, initially, I needed to use a washing-up bowl to collect water from the leaking roof through the ceiling. Those are now fixed and I feel honoured to live in such a lovely house.

I continue to work from home and travel quite a bit. I see my work as developing much more into encouraging others than being the pioneer. I realise that my experiences give me the right to speak into people's lives. I find myself supporting leaders in the justice field as they struggle with their own health challenges, vicarious trauma and burnout.

At the moment I am volunteering for over 90%+ of the work I do, and I work very hard. I would like to continue to do what I do without having to worry about finances. If you would like to financially support me please do so using this link:
stewardship.org.uk/partners/20390208

I enjoy painting with watercolours. I enjoy walking my dog Wally on the beach and at the local Cyne gardens. I enjoy hanging out with my daughter, her partner and my grandson. I enjoy meeting my others Zoe and Hannah when they come down or I go to them.

In the last couple of years I enjoy wearing much more colourful shirts and clothes. It's not drag but it does cause a few glances, some positive and others not so much.

Nevertheless, it hasn't been easy struggling with

personal health challenges, supporting my daughter Sarah and her health challenges and with the difficulties she has had in accessing her son/my grandson. We constantly remind each other that we love each other.

As I have written my story I realise that there are a number of times I might have died but God hasn't done with me yet.

I sometimes think about the actual time I have left. My life expectancy for someone of my current age in the UK is around 83 which means I have 20 years left. How will I spend it to make the most of that time? If I lived in a slum in Asia I would most already likely be at the end of my life expectancy now. How will I survive into old age? I know that I have a higher chance of health challenges with my previous head injury and auto-immune diseases and this may shorten that period but what if I am fortunate enough to have OK health for the next 20 years? I want to use it well.

I would like to find a male partner to love and be loved by. I would like to continue to encourage others to do justice work and look out for those who are the real survivors. I would like to do a little more travelling for fun (rather than work) and visit places I haven't yet seen such as the temples of Myanmar, the pyramids of Egypt and a safari in Kenya. I would like to see my grandson grow into a man who is confident in himself, kind and thoughtful and acquires a faith. I would like to continue to thrive in Mumbles and the Gower peninsula with its amazing beauty.

I want to see an end to the silence around sexual abuse and human trafficking. I want to see a world where the minority North is aware of the needs of the majority South and is willing to make sacrifices to work alongside them to find the solutions needed to reduce poverty and discrimination. I want to see a church that reaches out to include everyone.

It is time to share my story and help others to tell theirs.

Most biographies are written in an upward trajectory where it ends with everything hunky dory but my life continues to go in ups and downs. I am still healing from the abuse that happened 50 years ago. Mountains and Valleys. But in spite of it all, even to myself, I am a surprisingly strong survivor. My story isn't finished yet.

Reflection:

How will you use the rest of your life? What do you think God/a higher power wants you to do for him and the world?

Resources:

- Mumbles and the Gower: <u>visitwales.com/destinations/west-wales/swansea-bay/exploring-gower-peninsula</u>
- *Stewardship Foundation*: If you want to contribute a personal gift to me for my work to help pay for research, travel and expenses: stewardship.org.uk/partners/20390208

Or scan me instead!

Glenn Miles PhD was sexually abused as a child and came out publicly as a gay man when he was sixty. In between these two major events, he lived an extraordinary life facing many serious personal challenges but became an advocate and researcher with some of the most vulnerable people on the planet.

POWERFUL BOOKS

Powerful Books was born in February 2023 with the aim of empowering trauma survivors to find deep healing, find their voice, and impact others with their story. Because of that, we approach publishing in a different way. Along with the community, group coaching, and self-paced course, we provide everything a trauma survivor needs to go from blank page to published book in just 3-6 months.

Our aim is to be one of the most impactful publishing companies in the world, creating ripples of impact through the stories of inspiring trauma survivors.

For more information head on over to www.powerfulbooks.co.uk.

Printed in Great Britain
by Amazon